# Learning iOS Security

Enhance the security of your iOS platform and applications using iOS-centric security techniques

**Allister Banks**

**Charles S. Edge**

[PACKT] open source*
PUBLISHING community experience distilled

BIRMINGHAM - MUMBAI

# Learning iOS Security

First published: February 2015

Production reference: 2240215

Published by Packt Publishing Ltd.
Livery Place
35 Livery Street
Birmingham B3 2PB, UK.

ISBN 978-1-78355-174-3

www.packtpub.com

# Credits

**Authors**
Allister Banks
Charles S. Edge

**Reviewers**
Jeremy Agostino
William Smith

**Commissioning Editor**
Ashwin Nair

**Acquisition Editor**
Hemal Desai

**Content Development Editor**
Mamata Walkar

**Technical Editor**
Menza Mathew

**Copy Editors**
Jasmine Nadar
Wishva Shah

**Project Coordinator**
Shipra Chawhan

**Proofreaders**
Safis Editing
Paul Hindle

**Indexer**
Tejal Soni

**Production Coordinator**
Melwyn D'sa

**Cover Work**
Melwyn D'sa

# About the Authors

**Allister Banks** is an enthusiast. He's very excited to be in the exceedingly limited, exclusive club of coauthors of Charles S. Edge. After working for a decade with IT consulting companies on both the coasts of the U.S., he now works for a medical-focused institution with education and data center aspects. He has given speeches at LOPSA-East, MacTech Conference, and MacAdmins Conference at Penn State. He lives in New York. He contributes to various open source projects and speaks enough Japanese to order food.

**Charles S. Edge** has been working with Apple products since he was a child. Professionally, Charles started with the Mac OS and Apple server offerings in 1999 after working of years with various flavors of Unix. Charles began his consulting career with Support Technologies and Andersen Consulting. As the chief technology officer of 318, Inc., a consulting firm in Santa Monica, California, Charles built and nurtured a team of over 50 engineers, which was the largest Mac team in the world at that time. Charles is now a product manager at JAMF Software, with a focus on Bushel (`http://www.bushel.com`).

Charles has spoken at a variety of conferences including DefCon, BlackHat, LinuxWorld, MacWorld, MacSysAdmin, and Apple Worldwide Developers Conference. Charles has also written 12 books, over 3,000 blog posts, and a number of printed articles on Apple products.

# About the Reviewers

**Jeremy Agostino** is a longtime Mac and iOS developer with a professional focus on hardware support and device drivers. He has assisted in the design and implementation of custom technical solutions to manage some of the largest iOS deployments in the U.S. Jeremy is currently leading the engineering team at Ground Control Solutions, where he is developing a powerful deployment and management tool for iOS devices.

**William Smith** is a solutions architect for 318, Inc., which is an IT consultancy that is based in Santa Monica, California. He is a technology veteran with more than 20 years of experience. He lives in Saint Paul, Minnesota, where he has provided training and consulting services on behalf of customers such as Apple and JAMF Software.

William enjoys writing and presenting on technology topics and he has spoken at JAMF Nation User Conference, MacIT, PSU MacAdmins, and other conferences. He has been a Microsoft MVP for more than 11 years and is co-owner of OfficeforMacHelp. com. Currently, he is a part of the steering committee for the new Twin Cities Mac Admins professionals group—a community that supports all things Apple, from education to enterprise.

# www.PacktPub.com

## Support files, eBooks, discount offers, and more

For support files and downloads related to your book, please visit www.PacktPub.com.

Did you know that Packt offers eBook versions of every book published, with PDF and ePub files available? You can upgrade to the eBook version at www.PacktPub.com and as a print book customer, you are entitled to a discount on the eBook copy. Get in touch with us at service@packtpub.com for more details.

At www.PacktPub.com, you can also read a collection of free technical articles, sign up for a range of free newsletters and receive exclusive discounts and offers on Packt books and eBooks.

https://www2.packtpub.com/books/subscription/packtlib

Do you need instant solutions to your IT questions? PacktLib is Packt's online digital book library. Here, you can search, access, and read Packt's entire library of books.

## Why subscribe?

- Fully searchable across every book published by Packt
- Copy and paste, print, and bookmark content
- On demand and accessible via a web browser

## Free access for Packt account holders

If you have an account with Packt at www.PacktPub.com, you can use this to access PacktLib today and view 9 entirely free books. Simply use your login credentials for immediate access.

# Table of Contents

# Preface

Nowadays, iOS is becoming more and more prevalent in companies and larger organizations. Whether this is a trend that is driven by Bring Your Own Device (BYOD) or something that is coming from within the IT department, our knowledge of platforms is being stretched more and more all the time. It's getting harder and harder to be an expert on every platform that is in use in our organizations!

You need to secure your iOS devices. Learning iOS security gives you the knowledge to build security into large-scale iOS deployments. This book takes you through good security practices; these include configuring privacy options to keep personal data away from prying eyes, learning about encryption options to keep data safe at rest, securing apps to reduce the risks introduced by third-party apps, and then laying down practical steps and procedures for carrying out these steps, both on-screen on devices and at scale using Apple Configurator, profiles, and Mobile Device Management (MDM) solutions.

This book also includes a section on debugging and viewing data so that you can check out how to further secure items not covered in detail in the book. We teach you how to provide enterprise-class security to your iPhone, iPad, and iPod Touch deployments. This includes a quick run-down of basic security steps and mass deployment of these steps to aid in your large-scale deployment of iOS devices.

This book is meant to be an easy-to-digest guide that follows real-world examples to implement best security practices. Each topic is covered in a theoretical context and further resources are provided where they are needed/applicable.

# What this book covers

*Chapter 1, iOS Security Overview*, is a quick-and-dirty overview of the many steps to take to initially secure an iPad, iPhone, and iPod Touch. The purpose of this chapter isn't to go into too much depth with any given technology, but to provide a cheat sheet of sorts to get you started with iOS security.

*Chapter 2, Introducing App Security*, is a more thorough review of how to choose apps and secure them during an iOS deployment. Here, we look at an overview of sandboxing techniques and how to use Single App Mode and keybags. We also look at in-house Apps.

*Chapter 3, Encrypting Devices*, explains the encryption types and techniques that are used in iOS. Here, we look at Touch ID, Apple Pay, network encryption, and privacy concerns.

*Chapter 4, Organizational Controls*, introduces Apple Configurator and profile management. Here, we also look at the Find My iPhone app as it pertains to Activation Lock, ActiveSync policies (EAS Policies), and device supervision.

*Chapter 5, Mobile Device Management*, looks at Apple's Profile Manager and a simple third-party MDM called Bushel. Here, we look at Over the Air (OTA) profile management.

*Chapter 6, Debugging and Conclusion*, covers ways to troubleshoot and debug devices in larger deployments. In this chapter, we'll look at how to find logs and interpret them, how to get more data than you can use from devices, and then we will wrap up the book.

# What you need for this book

This book focuses on using a Mac to manage Apple iOS devices. Therefore, you should have a Mac that runs OS X 10.10 or a higher version and an iOS device that runs iOS 8 or a higher version. You can use a Windows or Linux computer instead of a Mac, but not all of the content covered in this book will be applicable if you do this.

# Who this book is for

This book is intended for systems administrators and security professionals who want to learn how to implement good security practices on iOS devices. The readers should know something about the Information Technology industry, but they need not be veterans who have an experience of more than 30 years.

# Conventions

In this book, you will find a number of styles of text that distinguish between different kinds of information. Here are some examples of these styles, and an explanation of their meaning.

Code words in text, database table names, folder names, filenames, file extensions, pathnames, dummy URLs, user input, and Twitter handles are shown as follows: "While not exactly simple, one could use openssl on various operating systems, in tandem with a root certificate from a trusted certificate authority, to apply signatures to configuration profiles, which devices will then see as trusted."

Any command-line input or output is written as follows:

```
codesign -d -vv /Users/abanks/Music/iTunes/iTunes\ Media/Mobile\
Applications/Dropbox\ 3.5.2/Payload/Dropbox.app
```

**New terms** and **important words** are shown in bold. Words that you see on the screen, in menus or dialog boxes for example, appear in the text like this: "This is exposed to end users with a **Send All Traffic** slider when optional.

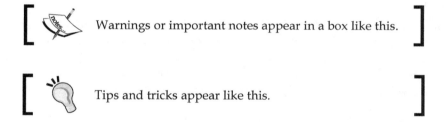

Warnings or important notes appear in a box like this.

Tips and tricks appear like this.

# Reader feedback

Feedback from our readers is always welcome. Let us know what you think about this book—what you liked or may have disliked. Reader feedback is important for us to develop titles that you really get the most out of.

To send us general feedback, simply send an e-mail to feedback@packtpub.com, and mention the book title via the subject of your message.

If there is a topic that you have expertise in and you are interested in either writing or contributing to a book, see our author guide on www.packtpub.com/authors.

# Customer support

Now that you are the proud owner of a Packt book, we have a number of things to help you to get the most from your purchase.

## Errata

Although we have taken every care to ensure the accuracy of our content, mistakes do happen. If you find a mistake in one of our books—maybe a mistake in the text or the code—we would be grateful if you would report this to us. By doing so, you can save other readers from frustration and help us improve subsequent versions of this book. If you find any errata, please report them by visiting http://www.packtpub.com/submit-errata, selecting your book, clicking on the **errata submission form** link, and entering the details of your errata. Once your errata are verified, your submission will be accepted and the errata will be uploaded on our website, or added to any list of existing errata, under the Errata section of that title. Any existing errata can be viewed by selecting your title from http://www.packtpub.com/support.

## Piracy

Piracy of copyright material on the Internet is an ongoing problem across all media. At Packt, we take the protection of our copyright and licenses very seriously. If you come across any illegal copies of our works, in any form, on the Internet, please provide us with the location address or website name immediately so that we can pursue a remedy.

Please contact us at copyright@packtpub.com with a link to the suspected pirated material.

We appreciate your help in protecting our authors, and our ability to bring you valuable content.

## Questions

You can contact us at questions@packtpub.com if you are having a problem with any aspect of the book, and we will do our best to address it.

# 1
# iOS Security Overview

Out of the box, iOS is one of the most secure operating systems available. There are a number of factors that contribute to the elevated security level. These include the fact that users cannot access the underlying operating system. Apps also have data in a silo (sandbox), so instead of accessing the system's internals they can access the silo. App developers choose whether to store settings such as passwords in the app or on iCloud Keychain, which is a secure location for such data on a device. Finally, Apple has a number of controls in place on devices to help protect users while providing an elegant user experience.

However, devices can be made even more secure than they are now. In this chapter, we're going to get some basic security tasks under our belt in order to get some basic best practices of security. Where we feel more explanation is needed about what we did on devices, we'll explore the technology itself either in this chapter, or others.

This chapter will cover the following topics:

- Pairing
- Backing up your device
- Initial security checklist
- Safari and built-in app protection
- Predictive search and spotlight

To kick off the overview of iOS security, we'll quickly secure our systems by initially providing a simple checklist of tasks, where we'll configure a few device protections that we feel everyone should use. Then, we'll look at how to take a backup of our devices and finally, at how to use a built-in web browser and protections around a browser.

# Pairing

When you connect a device to a computer that runs iTunes for the first time, you are prompted to enter a password. Doing so allows you to synchronize the device to a computer. Applications that can communicate over this channel include iTunes, iPhoto, Xcode, and others.

To pair a device to a Mac, simply plug the device in (if you have a passcode, you'll need to enter that in order to pair the device.) When the device is plugged in, you'll be prompted on both the device and the computer to establish a trust. Simply tap on **Trust** on the iOS device, as shown in the following screenshot:

Trusting a computer

For the computer to communicate with the iOS device, you'll also need to accept the pairing on your computer (although, when you use `libimobiledevice`, which is the command to pair, does not require doing so, because you use the command line to accept. This command is covered in *Chapter 6, Debugging and Conclusion*). When prompted, click on **Continue** to establish the pairing, as seen in the following screenshot (the screenshot is the same in Windows):

Trusting a device

When a device is paired, a file is created in `/var/db/lockdown`, which is the UDID of the device with a property list (`plist`) extension. A property list is an Apple XML file that stores a variety of attributes. In Windows, iOS data is stored in the `MobileSync` folder, which you can access by navigating to `\Users\(username)\AppData\Roaming\Apple Computer\MobileSync`. The information in this file sets up a trust between the computers and includes the following attributes:

- `DeviceCertificate`: This certificate is unique to each device.
- `EscrowBag`: The keybag of `EscrowBag` contains class keys used to decrypt the device.
- `HostCertificate`: This certificate is for the host who's paired with iOS devices (usually, the same for all files that you've paired devices with, on your computer).
- `HostID`: This is a generated ID for the host.
- `HostPrivateKey`: This is the private key for your Mac (should be the same in all files on a given computer).
- `RootCertificate`: This is the certificate used to generate keys (should be the same in all files on a given computer).
- `RootPrivateKey`: This is the private key of the computer that runs iTunes for that device.
- `SystemBUID`: This refers to the ID of the computer that runs iTunes.
- `WiFiMACAddress`: This is the Mac address of the Wi-Fi interface of the device that is paired to the computer. If you do not have an active Wi-Fi interface, MAC is still used while pairing.

Why does this matter? It's important to know how a device interfaces with a computer. These files can be moved between computers and contain a variety of information about a device, including private keys.

Having keys isn't all that is required for a computer to communicate with a device. When the devices are interfacing with a computer over USB, if you have a passcode enabled on the device, you will be required to enter that passcode in order to unlock the device.

Once a computer is able to communicate with a device, you need to be careful as the backups of a device, apps that get synchronized to a device, and other data that gets exchanged with a device can be exposed while at rest on devices.

# Backing up your device

What do most people do to maximize the security of iOS devices? Before we do anything, we need to take a backup of our devices. This protects the device from us by providing a restore point. This also secures the data from the possibility of losing it through a silly mistake. There are two ways, which are most commonly used to take backups: iCloud and iTunes. As the names imply, the first makes backups for the data on Apple's cloud service and the second on desktop computers.

We'll cover how to take a backup on iCloud first.

## iCloud backups

An iCloud account comes with free storage, to back up your Apple devices. An iOS device takes a backup to Apple servers and can be restored when a new device is set up from those same servers (it's a screen that appears during the activation process of a new device. Also, it appears as an option in iTunes if you back up to iTunes over USB—covered later in this chapter).

Setting up and checking the status of iCloud backups is a straightforward process. From the **Settings** app, tap on **iCloud** and then **Backup**. As you can see from the **Backup** screen, you have two options, **iCloud Backup**, which enables automatic backups of the device to your iCloud account, and **Back Up Now**, which runs an immediate backup of the device.

iCloud backups

Allowing iCloud to take backups on devices is optional. As you'll see in *Chapter 5, Mobile Device Management,* and *Chapter 6, Debugging and Conclusion,* you can disable access to iCloud and iCloud backups. However, doing so is rarely a good idea as you are limiting the functionality of the device and putting the data on your device at risk, if that data isn't backed up another way such as through iTunes. Many people have reservations about storing data on public clouds; especially, data as private as phone data (texts, phone call history, and so on). For more information on Apple's security and privacy around iCloud, refer to `http://support.apple.com/en-us/HT202303`. If you do not trust Apple or its cloud, then you can also take a backup of your device using iTunes, described in the next section.

## Taking backups using iTunes

Originally, iTunes was used to take backups for iOS devices. You can still use iTunes and it's likely you will have a second backup even if you are using iCloud, simply for a quick restore if nothing else.

Backups are usually pretty small. The reason is that the operating system is not part of backups, since users can't edit any of those files. Therefore, you can use an `ipsw` file (the operating system) to restore a device.

These are accessed through Apple Configurator (which is covered further in *Chapter 4, Organizational Controls*), or through iTunes if you have a restore file waiting to be installed. These can be seen in ~/Library/iTunes, and the name of the device and its software updates, as can be seen in the following screenshot:

| Name | ^ | Date Modified | Size |
|---|---|---|---|
| 🗋 https_buy.itunes.apple.com_0.localstorage | | Sep 29, 2014, 10:39 AM | 12 KB |
| 🗋 https_p7-buy.itune....com_0.localstorage | | Jul 11, 2014, 11:08 AM | 12 KB |
| ▼ 📁 iPad Software Updates | | Sep 18, 2014, 9:20 PM | -- |
| ▼ 📁 iPhone Software Updates | | Oct 20, 2014, 8:39 PM | -- |
| 🎯 iPhone6,1_8.1_12B411_Restore.ipsw | | Oct 20, 2014, 8:39 PM | 2.09 GB |
| ▼ 📁 iTunes Plug-ins | | Jun 2, 2014, 9:27 PM | -- |
| 🗋 StorageTracker.db | | Sep 29, 2014, 10:39 AM | 12 KB |

IPSW files

Backups are stored in the ~/Library/Application Support/MobileSync/Backup directory. Here, you'll see a number of directories that are associated with the UDID of the devices, and within those, you'll see a number of files that make up the modular incremental backups beyond the initial backup. It's a pretty smart system and allows you to restore a device at different points in time without taking too long to perform each backup.

Backups are stored in the \Documents and Settings\USERNAME\Application Data\Apple Computer\MobileSync\Backup\ directory on Windows XP and in the \Users\USERNAME\AppData\Roaming\Apple Computer\MobileSync\Backup\ directory for newer operating systems.

To enable an iTunes back up, plug a device into a computer, and then open iTunes. Click on the device for it to show the device details screen. The top section of the screen is for **Backups** (in the following screenshot, you can set a back up to **This computer**, which takes a backup on the computer you are on).

I would recommend you to always choose the **Encrypt iPhone backup** option as it forces you to save a password in order to restore the back up.

Additionally, you can use the **Back Up Now** button to kick off the first back up, as shown in the following screenshot:

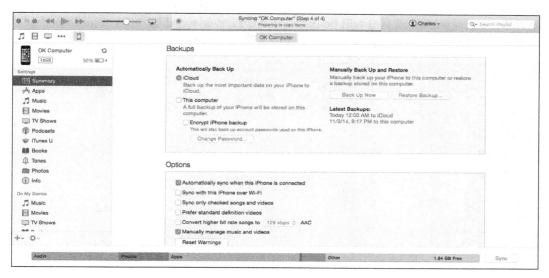

iTunes

# Viewing iOS data in iTunes

To show why it's important to encrypt backups, let's look at what can be pulled out of those backups. There are a few tools that can extract backups, provided you have a password. Here, we'll look at **iBackup Extractor** to view the backup of your browsing history, calendars, call history, contacts, iMessages, notes, photos, and voicemails.

To get started, download **iBackup Extractor** from `http://www.wideanglesoftware.com/ibackupextractor`. When you open **iBackup Extractor** for the first time, simply choose the device backup you wish to extract in **iBackup Extractor**. As you can see in following screenshot, you will be prompted for a password in order to unlock the **Backup keybag**. Enter the password to unlock the system.

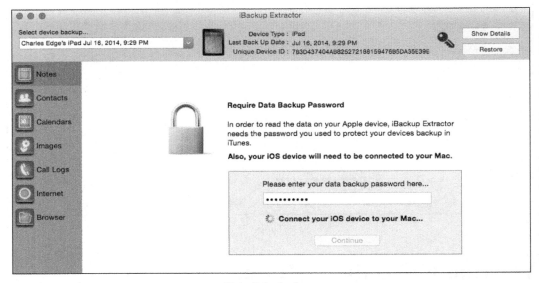

Unlock the backups

Note that the file tree in the following screenshot gives away some information on the structure of the iOS filesystem, or at least, the data stored in the backups of the iOS device, which we'll cover in detail in *Chapter 6, Debugging and Conclusion*. For now, simply click on **Browser** to see a list of files that can be extracted from the backup, as you can see in the next screenshot:

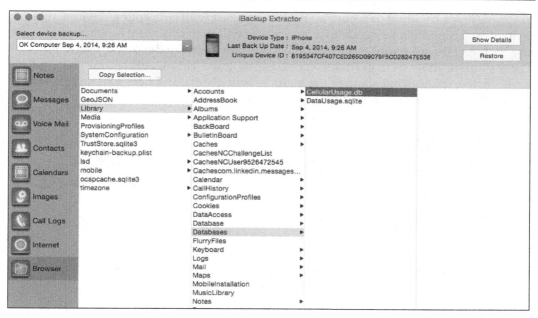

View device contents using iBackup Extractor

Note the prevalence of SQL databases in the files. Most apps use these types of databases to store data on devices. Also, check out the other options such as extracting notes (many that were possibly deleted), texts (some that have been deleted from devices), and other types of data from devices.

Now that we've exhausted backups and proven that you should really put a password in place for your back ups, let's finally get to some basic security tasks to be performed on these devices!

# Initial security checklist

Apple has built iOS to be one of the most secure operating systems in the world. This has been made possible by restricting access to much of the operating system by end users, unless you jailbreak a device. In this book, we don't cover jail-breaking devices much due to the fact that securing the devices then becomes a whole new topic. Instead, we have focused on what you need to do, how you can do those tasks, what the impacts are, and, how to manage security settings based on a policy.

The basic steps required to secure an iOS device start with encrypting devices, which is done by assigning a passcode to a device. We will then configure how much inactive time before a device requires a PIN and accordingly manage the privacy settings. These settings allow us to get some very basic security features under our belt, and set the stage to explain what some of the features actually do, and how we can set them via a policy in subsequent chapters of this book.

# Configuring a passcode

The first thing most of us need to do on an iOS device is configure a passcode for the device. Several things happen when a passcode is enabled, as shown in the following steps:

1. The device is encrypted.
2. The device then requires a passcode to wake up.
3. An idle timeout is automatically set that puts the device to sleep after a few minutes of inactivity.

This means that three of the most important things you can do to secure a device are enabled when you set up a passcode.

Best of all, Apple recommends setting up a passcode during the initial set up of new devices. You can manage passcode settings using policies (or profiles as Apple likes to call them in iOS), which we will cover in *Chapter 4*, *Organizational Controls*, and *Chapter 5*, *Mobile Device Management*.

Best of all—you can set a passcode and then use your fingerprint on the Home button instead of that passcode. We have found that by the time our phone is out of our pocket and if our finger is on the home button, the device is unlocked by the time we check it. With iPhone 6 and higher versions, you can now use that same fingerprint to secure payment information, which is covered in *Chapter 2*, *Introducing App Security*.

Check whether a passcode has been configured, and if needed, configure a passcode using the **Settings** app. The **Settings** app is by default on the Home screen where many settings on the device, including Wi-Fi networks the device has been joined to, app preferences, mail accounts, and other settings are configured.

- To set a passcode, open the **Settings** app and tap on **Touch ID & Passcode**
- If a passcode has been set, you will see the **Turn Passcode Off** (as seen in the following screenshot) option
- If a passcode has not been set, then you can do so at this screen as well

- Additionally, you can change a passcode that has been set using the **Change Passcode** button and define a fingerprint or additional fingerprints that can be used with a touch ID

There are two options in the **USE TOUCH ID FOR** section of the screen. You can choose whether, or not, you need to enter the passcode in order to unlock a phone, which you should use unless the device is also used by small children or as a kiosk. In these cases, you don't need to encrypt or take a backup of the device anyway. The second option is to force the entering of a passcode while using the App Store and iTunes. This can cost you money if someone else is using your device, so let the default value remain, which requires you to enter a passcode to unlock the options.

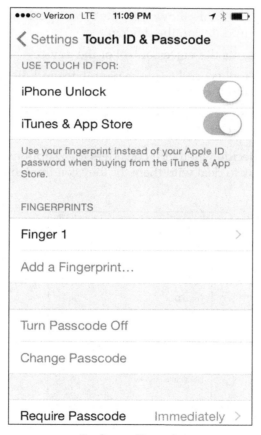

Configure a Passcode

The passcode settings are very easy to configure; so, they should be configured when possible. Scroll down on this screen and you'll see several other features, as shown in the next screenshot. The first option on the screen is **Simple Passcode**. Most users want to use a simple pin with an iOS device. Trying to use alphanumeric and long passcodes simply causes most users to try to circumvent the requirement. To add a fingerprint as a passcode, simply tap on **Add a Fingerprint…**, which you can see in the preceding screenshot, and follow the onscreen instructions.

Additionally, the following can be accessed when the device is locked, and you can choose to turn them off:

- **Today**: This shows an overview of upcoming calendar items
- **Notifications View**: This shows you the recent push notifications (apps that have updates on the device)
- **Siri**: This represents the voice control of the device
- **Passbook**: This tool is used to make payments and display tickets for concert venues and meetups
- **Reply with Message**: This tool allows you to send a text reply to an incoming call (useful if you're on the treadmill)

Each organization can decide whether it considers these options to be a security risk and direct users how to deal with them, or they can implement a policy around these options.

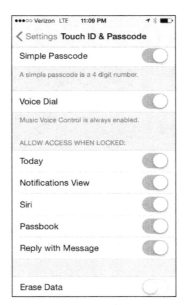

Passcode Settings

There aren't a lot of security options around passcodes and encryption because by and large, Apple secures the device by giving you fewer options than you'll actually use. Under the hood, (for example through Apple Configurator and Mobile Device Management, covered in *Chapter 4, Organizational Controls* and *Chapter 5, Mobile Device Management*, respectively) there are a lot of other options, but these aren't exposed to end users of devices. For the most part, a simple four-character passcode will suffice for most environments. When you complicate passcodes, devices become much more difficult to unlock, and users tend to look for ways around passcode enforcement policies. The passcode is only used on the device, so complicating the passcode will only reduce the likelihood that a passcode would be guessed before swiping open a device, which typically occurs within 10 tries.

Finally, to disable a passcode and therefore encryption, simply go to the **Touch ID & Passcode** option in the **Settings** app and tap on **Turn Passcode Off**.

# Configuring privacy settings

Once a passcode is set and the device is encrypted, it's time to configure the privacy settings. Third-party apps cannot communicate with one another by default in iOS. Therefore, you must enable communication between them (also between third-party apps and built-in iOS apps that have APIs). This is a fundamental concept when it comes to securing iOS devices.

To configure privacy options, open the **Settings** app and tap on the entry for **Privacy**. On the **Privacy** screen, you'll see a list of each app that can be communicated with by other apps, as shown in the following screenshot:

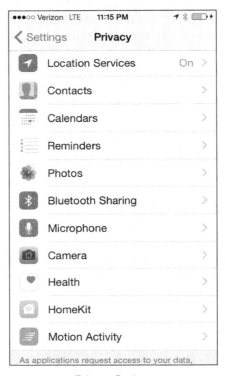

Privacy Options

As an example, tap on the **Location Services** entry, as shown in the next screenshot. Here, you can set which apps can communicate with **Location Services** and when. If an app is set to **While Using**, the app can communicate with **Location Services** when the app is open. If an app is set to **Always**, then the app can only communicate with **Location Services** when the app is open and not when it runs in the background.

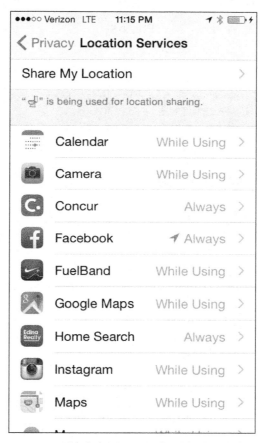

Configure Location Services

On the **Privacy** screen, tap on **Photos**. Here, you have fewer options because unlike the location of a device, you can't access photos when the app is running in the background. Here, you can enable or disable an app by communicating with the photo library on a device, as seen in the next screenshot:

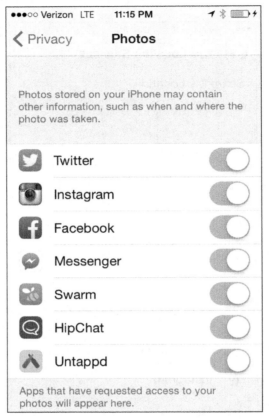

Configure what Apps can access your Camera Roll

Each app should be configured in such a way that it can communicate with the features of iOS or other apps that are absolutely necessary.

Other privacy options which you can consider disabling include Siri and Handoff. Siri has the voice controls of an iOS. Because Siri can be used even when your phone is locked, consider to disable it by opening the **Settings** app, tapping on **General** and then on **Siri**, and you will be able disable the voice controls. To disable Handoff, you should use the **General System Preference** pane in any OS X computer paired to an iOS device. There, uncheck the **Allow Handoff between this Mac and your iCloud devices** option.

# Safari and built-in App protections

Web browsers have access to a lot of data. One of the most popular targets on other platforms has been web browsers. The default browser on an iOS device is Safari.

Open the **Settings** app and then tap on **Safari**. The Safari preferences to secure iOS devices include the following:

- **Passwords & AutoFill**: This is a screen that includes contact information, a list of saved passwords and credit cards used in web browsers. This data is stored in an iCloud Keychain if iCloud Keychain has been enabled in your phone.

- **Favorites**: This performs the function of bookmark management. This shows bookmarks in iOS.

- **Open Links**: This configures how links are managed.

- **Block Pop-ups**: This enables a pop-up blocker.

Scroll down and you'll see the **Privacy & Security** options (as seen in the next screenshot). Here, you can do the following:

- **Do Not Track**: By this, you can block the tracking of browsing activity by websites.

- **Block Cookies**: A cookie is a small piece of data sent from a website to a visitor's browser. Many sites will send cookies to third-party sites, so the management of cookies becomes an obstacle to the privacy of many. By default, Safari only allows cookies from websites that you visit (**Allow from Websites I Visit**). Set the **Cookies** option to **Always Block** in order to disable its ability to accept any cookies; set the option to **Always Allow** to accept cookies from any source; and set the option to **Allow from Current Website Only** to only allow cookies from certain websites.

- **Fraudulent Website Warning**: This blocks phishing attacks (sites that only exist to steal personal information).

- **Clear History and Website Data**: This clears any cached history, web files, and passwords from the Safari browser.

- **Use Cellular Data**: When this option is turned off, it disables web traffic over cellular connections (so web traffic will only work when the phone is connected to a Wi-Fi network).

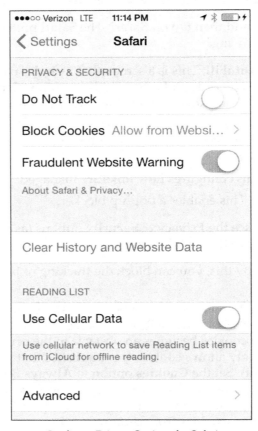

Configure Privacy Settings for Safari

There are also a number of advanced options that can be accessed by clicking on the **Advanced** button, as shown in the following screenshot:

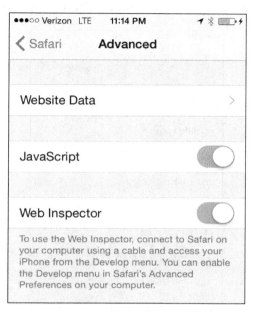

Configure the **Advanced** Safari Options

These advanced options include the following:

- **Website Data**: This option (as you can see in the next screenshot) shows the amount of data stored from each site that caches files on the device, and allows you to swipe left on these entries to access any files saved for the site. Tap on **Remove All Website Data** to remove data for all the sites at once.

- **JavaScript**: This allows you to disable any JavaScripts from running on sites the device browses.

- **Web Inspector**: This shows the device in the **Develop** menu on a computer connected to the device. If the **Web Inspector** option has been disabled, use **Advanced Preferences** in the **Safari Preferences** option of Safari.

View website data on devices

Browser security is an important aspect of any operating system.

# Predictive search and spotlight

The final aspect of securing the settings on an iOS device that we'll cover in this chapter includes predictive search and spotlight. When you use the spotlight feature in iOS, usage data is sent to Apple along with the information from Location Services. Additionally, you can search for anything on a device, including items previously blocked from being accessed. The ability to search for blocked content warrants the inclusion in locking down a device.

That data is then used to generate future searches. This feature can be disabled by opening the **Settings** app, tap on **Privacy**, then **Location Services**, and then **System Services**. Simply slide **Spotlight Suggestions** to **Off** to disable the location data from going over that connection. To limit the type of data that spotlight sends, open the **Settings** app, tap on **General**, and then on **Spotlight Search**. Uncheck each item you don't want indexed in the Spotlight database. The following screenshot shows the mentioned options:

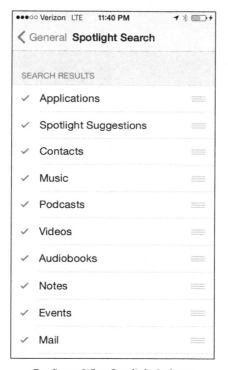

Configure What Spotlight Indexes

Now that we've looked at some basic tactical tasks that secure devices, it's time to turn our attention to the theory behind some of these and to make sure your apps are secure, in the next chapter.

# Summary

This chapter was a whirlwind of quick changes that secure a device. Here, we paired devices, took a backup, set a passcode, and secured app data and Safari. This is by far the simplest chapter of this book, but also lays the groundwork to cover some of the more esoteric content. In this chapter, we showed how to manually do some tasks that we will set via policies later in the book.

In the next chapter, we will move on to securing apps and learn how apps communicate with one another.

# 2

# Introducing App Security

In this chapter, we will look at one of the most important things to secure on iOS: apps. This includes data within apps, the context in which apps are allowed to run, how apps communicate via extensions, and how newer features in OS continue to put the focus on an Apple ID as the most important account to control on your device. However, the reason why most people sign up for an Apple ID is to install apps.

Many of the concepts discussed in this chapter will be an addition to or a reinforcement of our knowledge about the OS X architecture upon which iOS is based, which will be especially helpful if you are coming from the Windows or Blackberry platforms. Even Linux, with its process model echoing Unix, still has enough notable differences with the **appliance**-style computing experience showcased on iOS that it will be helpful to cover these more fundamental points. We will also briefly touch on in-house app development, which can be augmented by the management systems that we will be discussing in *Chapter 4, Organizational Controls*, and *Chapter 5, Mobile Device Management*.

The topics that we will cover in this chapter, which underpin app security, include:

- How apps are distributed, installed, and restricted
- Single app mode (also known as **Lock to App**) and **Guided Access**
- Traditional and current inter-app (and device) communication
- Clarification of when keybags are utilized by iOS
- Keyboards, sandboxing, and extensions
- Introduction to securely distributing custom in-house apps

# Installing apps

How to install an app is considered a trivial exercise at this point, with common advertisements doing nothing more than showing the icons of the platform to suggest that they want you to get their app from the corresponding store. That being said, there are other ways to download and install an app than simply opening an app store on a device and tapping on **Get**. An app can be pushed over the air with management systems, put on the device with tools such as Apple Configurator (discussed in *Chapter 4, Organizational Controls*), and installed once it is compiled from the source code with Xcode (Apple's **Integrated Development Environment (IDE)**, which is discussed with other tools that can perform installations in *Chapter 6, Debugging and Conclusion*).

There is no concept of sideloading apps on iOS in comparison to other platforms where you may be able to place a device into developer mode. Likewise you will likely never have implicit or otherwise stated encouragement to gain root access to the device. We'll discover the lengths to which Apple goes to ensure this in the next chapter, but suffice it to say that you simply cannot transfer a binary to an iOS device and bring about a system-wide change in any but the endorsed ways while playing within Apple's so-called **walled garden**.

Apps themselves can only be distributed by Apple via the App Store that's available on the device, and in iTunes on a Mac or PC, through a special Business-to-Business store with the Volume Purchase Program, or when explicitly associated with an Apple Developer Program. These limited options decrease the routes through which applications can be acquired, but if you have a developer account, you can compile applications released as open source and install them on devices at will. Similarly, the compressed .ipa archive that contains an iOS application can be transferred like any data, but getting the installer process in the OS to pick up on it is another matter.

Security around app installation manifests itself in the fact that the kernel performs verification at installation time and every subsequent launch to ensure that the executable bundle and frameworks inside the archive have been signed with an approved developer's certificate that Apple trusts. There is no installer binary for IPA files on iOS, so verification like the one that is done with the pkg encapsulation format on the Mac is not a part of the process .As long as the code delivered by an archive checks out as signed, it is allowed to be installed and run. One can speculate that this allows more caching possibilities since there is less likelihood of corruption, as all you need to change is the **Digital Rights Management (DRM)** software upon delivery to a new device.

You can see the app signature verification process on a Mac using the following steps:

1. First, download an app from iTunes and navigate to it in the **Finder**. Normally, it can be found by navigating to `/Users/your username/Music/ iTunes/Mobile Applications`, Duplicate the file (if you'd like to keep a fresh, unaltered version) and highlight the copy. Then, from the **File** menu, choose **Open With | Archive Utility** to expand it.

2. You will then see a folder of the same name with several things inside it, one of which is a folder labeled **Payload**.

3. Launch the Terminal application that you will find in the **Other** folder in **Launchpad**. You would first type `codesign -d -vv` and then drag and drop the application you find inside the **Payload** folder, and then hit return. On executing the command, you will see something like the following:

```
codesign -d -vv /Users/abanks/Music/iTunes/iTunes\ Media/Mobile\
Applications/Dropbox\ 3.5.2/Payload/Dropbox.app

Executable=/Users/abanks/Music/iTunes/iTunes Media/Mobile
Applications/Dropbox 3.5.2/Payload/Dropbox.app/Dropbox

Identifier=com.getdropbox.Dropbox

Format=bundle with Mach-O universal (armv7 arm64)

CodeDirectory v=20200 size=54086 flags=0x0(none) hashes=2695+5
location=embedded

Signature size=3487

Authority=Apple iPhone OS Application Signing

Authority=Apple iPhone Certification Authority

Authority=Apple Root CA
```

An output such as the preceding one will appear, which will show the chain of trust in action. Apple's Root **Certificate Authority (CA)** is present as a trusted authority to verify that the application inside the `.ipa` file that we acquired has not been tampered with.

# Blocking access to the App Store

One can potentially hide the App Store application on the device, but if the device can still connect to an end users computer that is running iTunes, you will not be able to effectively cut off the installation of apps.

There have been additional, undocumented ways to hide features and apps that are actually present on a device in certain jurisdictions, most of which rely in some part on configuration profiles, but that is beyond the scope of this book.

As demonstrated by the access granted to data on the device by backing it up to a computer in the last chapter, when allowing end users to directly interact with the backup process, it should be thoroughly examined and accounted for in a written policy.

The most simplistic form of applying management to an iOS device is to navigate to **Settings** | **General** | **Restrictions**, tap on Enable Restrictions, and then set a new password that is distinct from the one used to unlock the device. Then, you can granularly disable **Installing Apps**, **Deleting Apps**, and **In-App Purchases** and essentially shut off all interactions with the apps on a device, as shown in the following figure:

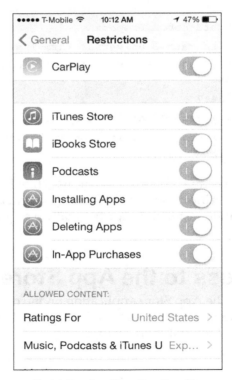

Restricting App Store Functionality

Management tools such as Apple Configurator and iTunes will also not be able to install or remove apps once these settings are enabled, which makes controlling access to Restrictions of particular importance to educational environments.

# Single App mode, App Lock, and Guided Access

When devices are made to work a shared-usage model, for example, many nurses using the same iPad during shifts at a hospital, one method to restrict access and standardize the experience would be to lock the device to a single app. This is referred to by different names based on how it is initiated, and it can be achieved with the tools that we will discuss in future chapters. The device shows only the designated app and never goes to the home screen (also referred to internally as the Springboard). The **Home** button is essentially disabled and Control Center (which is accessed by swiping up from the bottom edge of an iOS device) is also not accessible. This can also enable a kiosk-type experience, where the device is protected from misuse by dictating that only a single app can run.

In recent releases of iOS, developers have been granted APIs to enable app lock when they enter a certain state within the app or until a specific requirement is met; however, this is applicable only for apps distributed via **Mobile Device Management (MDM)**. This meets the criteria for educational use where you do not want students to look up answers. It can also prevent exfiltration of data within the apps on a device if you can coordinate with a developer to enable this feature. Financial processing, secure document viewing, and other sensitive app interaction may benefit from this as well.

You can simulate how a locked device will perform at any time by enabling a feature called **Guided Access**. You can initiate this mode by pressing the **Home** button three times from within an app. You will then be presented with options to control motion (the ability to rotate the screens' orientation) and the use of the keyboard. It detects screen elements, so you can designate specific regions of the screen to be off-limits, for example, the in-app purchase button or ads. Exiting **Guided Access** requires yet another distinct four-digit password, but it can be disabled with the fingerprint unlock feature on devices that are equipped with Touch ID.

You can find more information about this at `http://support.apple.com/HT202612`. The following screenshot shows the **Guided Access** configuration screen on an iPhone:

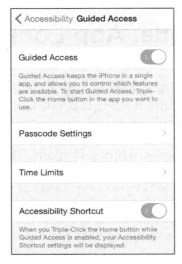

Enabling **Guided Access**

Now, the following screenshot shows how the controls of an app can be selectively disabled:

Disabling Controls in an App

One of the things that people utilizing this functionality discover as a support concern is that you cannot turn off the device nor put the screen in sleep mode. This makes powering the device of critical importance, as does ensuring a consistent Wi-Fi connection; there is no way to re-enter credentials or switch networks. The preceding screenshots show how you can enable **Guided Access** and what you would see when you configure it, whereas no configuration is presented when using MDM or in-app functionality to **Lock to App**; further restrictions may be necessary if you would like to disable in-app purchases or unnecessary web views.

 Documenting an obscure feature like **Guided Access** is actually quite a challenge, as the normal, simple to use screenshot controls on the device are effectively disabled. Instead of messing about with video capture via a physical adapter or cable, Apple's AirPlay feature can be paired with an app like Reflector by Squirrels (http://www.airsquirrels.com/reflector/) to mirror the screen to a Mac, PC, or an Android device from which you can then take screenshots.

# App communication

Historically, very few affordances were made when one developer wanted to communicate with the application data of another developer. URL schemes were manipulated for this purpose and they allowed a developer's app to be summoned by an identifier that was usually based on the bundle ID. In the last few major releases of iOS, there was at least the affordance for shared credentials to be accessed between apps by the same developer. This sharing of a **keychain** by an app group now also includes the sharing of file storage and preference data, which was previously accomplished by separate accounts with third-party sync services like Dropbox. iCloud Drive has been introduced to perform similar ad hoc file storage and sharing tasks. If this sounds somewhat limiting, it's because historically it has been, but we will touch upon the new ways in which app functionality and data can leak out from the one-app-at-a-time silo after we discuss how app data can now pass more easily between devices. The following screenshot shows a web page in Safari on an iOS 8 device that is being offered to a Mac running OS X 10.10:

A web page in Safari on an iOS 8 device that is being offered to a Mac running OS X 10.10

# Handoff and Continuity

Let's start by signing into the same Apple ID on a Mac running OS X 10.10 (Yosemite) and an iPhone or iPad running iOS 8. Open a web page in Safari on the iOS device and you will see an icon in your Dock (analogous to the taskbar on Windows) to continue viewing the web page on the Mac. This is **Handoff** in action. It's also referred to under the **Continuity** heading in Apple's marketing material. Many Apple apps are shipping with this functionality in iOS 8, and the developers of popular apps like Google's Chrome web browser are rapidly adopting it as well.

iCloud and the newest operating systems are the glue that hold all this together and these features work between iOS devices. For other **Continuity** features such as phone/text message relay, you may need to explicitly set up the relationship between devices when prompted, as shown in the following figure:

Authorizing an iPad to receive text messages (SMS and MMS)

As a troubleshooting step, make sure that any device that will piggyback on an iPhone's service is using the phone number of an iPhone and the e-mail address of the Apple ID to identify itself to iCloud-based services. You can find more details about this at `http://support.apple.com/HT6337`.

Some people have criticized this duplication of possibly redundant or sensitive application states across devices, which you would be automatically opted-in to use if you have an iPhone and which uses the same Apple ID and phone number as the primary identifier of iCloud-based services such as iMessage and FaceTime. This increases the moving parts that need to be secured and the importance of the device wipe feature that is present in ActiveSync, Find My iPhone, and the MDM-based enterprise wipe.

# Keybags and keychains

As discussed in the previous chapter, the keychain is known as a way to centrally store and manage credentials and other secret data that are in use by applications on the behalf of the user, carried over from OS X. There is also the concept of a **keybag**, which in practice is a grouping of secrets (or more practically, keys) that allow the system to manage the moving parts around specific interactions. Besides, when used by the system itself to manage the encryption of the data, these deal with primarily when a backup will run either over Wi-Fi to iTunes, when tethered by USB to iTunes, or while the device is plugged into a power source and locked as a requirement to send to iCloud Backup.

Explaining keybags as a concept is a minor point, but there has been terminology confusion regarding things such as the securing of apps with digital rights management and the use of the keychain, neither of which are directly related. To summarize, keybags are an abstraction for secrets like keychain items, so they can be secured independent of the data within. This allows for more flexible security by adding an interaction-specific layer to events such as the rotation of credentials, among other common interactions.

Some keychain items can be marked as tied to a specific device when they are created by an application, disallowing them from being restored to another device. Google appears to be using this in their popular two-step authentication app Google Authenticator, whereas other services do not impose this limitation.

# Keyboards and extensions

One of the greatly anticipated features of iOS 8 was the concept of **Extensions**. While shuttling around the state of an application is all well and good, extensions allow apps to have their functionality appear in new places.

This is implemented through the addition of specific abilities presented to developers that are referred to as extension points, with the most anticipated being third-party keyboards. A more popular keyboard that is available for other platforms is **Swype** (though I am personally waiting for the return of Palm's Graffiti), which allows more fluid, one-handed text entry.

Apple grouped other possible extension categories under **Today** widgets (**Today** being a newly expanded view in **Notification Center** on iOS and Mac), photo editing enhancements (for example, filters from popular apps like VSCO Cam), document providers for importing files from popular sync services like Dropbox, and share providers like the pre-existing but system provided Facebook sharing functionality. More broadly, the vaguely named **custom actions** allow apps to be interactive even when the screen is locked, and from within a small drop-down interface when they receive notifications while the screen is unlocked.

The security and privacy concerns that Apple has addressed for keyboards in particular are how inputs for password fields and network communication are handled, so that a keyboard app cannot send keystrokes over the network and become the least imposing-looking keylogger. Extensions are distributed in regular app bundles and follow common privacy and security controls. In addition, one must explicitly allow network traffic for a keyboard in **Settings**, but even Apple's own Predictive Text keyboard add-on cannot enter text in a designated ( properly coded) password field.

Note that much of the Apple Watch's preliminary app functionality is enabled via extensions and all the processing happens in the iPhone. These are then sent to the device over Bluetooth Low Energy. Very little is stored about an app on the watch itself (UI storyboards that can contain dynamically updating content like watch faces), so securing the iPhone will be sufficient.

# Securing what extensions can access

The ability to enforce these expanded privacy and network access controls was prepared by having interapplication communication (under the protocol name **XPC**) added as part of iOS 5 (and OS X 10.7). The specific APIs for this type of communication ensure that apps will not share the same file or memory space with an extension.

Essentially, both parties stay in their own sandbox but XPC arbitrates and acts as a proxy between them. In terms of Privacy, while any right granted to the extension's container app will be inherited by it, a new app will not share its privacy settings with another developer's extension that is accessible within it.

While we will discuss MDM in depth later, their use adds the potential to apply more on-the-fly controls, which include limiting the mail accounts through which data can be sent, or the sharing and document providers enabled on a device that data can be moved to. A lot of this also depends on the MDM actually supplying the applications, but this becomes very powerful when paired with an in-house app.

## User context

The old Unix security model, from when the only way for the average person to use a computer was by sharing time on a mainframe, stated that nobody was trusted except the system administrator. When one was given a standard user account to log in, there was only a limited range of things that one could do to introduce instability to the system. iOS and its precursor OS X are descendants of NeXT, and BSD before that. This puts the concept of system processes running under user accounts with their associated privileges into focus.

iOS runs apps on behalf of a standard user account named mobile, and unlike OS X, it doesn't help to enable an awareness of multiple users on the system. When using an iOS device, we do not think about traditional user accounts (there is no interface to add more users), as the design assumption is that there is only one owner of this highly personalized device and therefore, there is only one actual user. Role accounts that would run daemons on behalf of third-party application processes are absent, as what is allowed to run is strictly limited on iOS (as it is on a Mac now; with the many restrictions that have been imposed on the apps that are allowed in its corresponding App Store).

## Sandboxing and App data storage

As we mentioned in the beginning of the chapter, a code signature is placed on the app bundle itself with additional protection, so that the signature is verified not only when the app is installed, but also at runtime when the app is launched, to make sure that it has not been modified in the meantime. This is for stability as much as it is for security, since code that has been modified or allowed to run roughshod on the system can cause the device, which we might just want to be able to use to call 911 in an emergency, to crash.

We spoke about a mobile user which would have a home folder. Unlike the common consumer computer OS, the data storage location of an app is randomly generated and kept separate from the user (besides the containerization of specific preferences that help sharing among a developer's apps, so those settings persist even if an app is deleted). There are frameworks, which are shipped by Apple in its SDK, that encourage storing app data in an encrypted format. However, some exploits have used an impersonation of an app's bundle identifier to make it trustworthy to other applications that will be able to exchange data with it. To date, forensic deconstruction of these attempts has found that users must explicitly enable non-standard behavior through several extenuating circumstances for exploits to work. The potential for data leakage has not been substantial on non-jailbroken devices, but security professionals should be aware of this shortcoming where end users are involved in the installation of apps.

Plain file storage is not the only way in which data is segregated and treated discriminately on the system; other privacy or device usage-related permissions must be requested by an app through entitlements. The previously introduced extensions can be contrasted with Android intents, as they are both initiated by the end-user and are focused from that perspective (although Android apps tend to broadcast their capabilities to receive data without a strict or clear oversight, which some would argue is actually beneficial due to a perceived increases in productivity and functionality). Entitlements are only slightly different from Windows phone contracts, and Apple's stated model mentions that apps should ask for as few rights as possible, which end users should be (as unobtrusively as possible) prompted to explicitly grant access for, and even then, only when it is absolutely necessary for the full usage of an app's capabilities. These are specified in the application bundle and can be investigated with the `codesign` binary on a Mac.

# Introduction to in-house App development

So, you have found a need to deploy a custom app to the devices in your organization and have received the go-ahead to build one. Apple encourages organizations and their developers to sign up with its Enterprise Developer Program so that they can be granted the capability to build and distribute custom-built apps outside the App Store. Many IT departments have already signed up individuals to not only test a release of the operating system, but the tinkerers amongst us can also build open source apps for personal use, which can also be achieved with a standard, standalone developer account. You can find more information about this at https://developer.apple.com/enterprise/.

The process of tying the required certificates and identifiers for an app to the desired devices for testing is referred to as provisioning. Creating and managing provisioning profiles will not always be necessary; however, it depends on how close to in-house your actual development may be. When you use Apple's approval process to clear an in-house developed app for internal use, you will most often use the Business Volume Purchase program and leverage Apple's infrastructure to distribute it. This is by far the easiest way from a procurement and ongoing support perspective, and this is often the case for white-labeled apps that are made by professional app development companies. Apps in the Business-to-Business, Volume Purchase app store are not visible to the general public, which may also be beneficial depending on the situation.

Ad hoc distribution allows limited beta testing on registered devices. This requires all the same steps that an individual will perform to get an app on the App Store, including registering as a developer, applying to have their app ID considered as unique, acquiring the correct certificates so that devices trust the app when it is installed, and preparing the built application for deployment once all the mentioned requirements are complete. You will additionally need to go through the process of building a team entity to identify the developers working on your behalf and grant them access to your account when they build the applications. When it comes to wider testing with many devices, Apple has recently acquired an outside service called *TestFlight* that makes this process easier for a large number of testers, although a number of other solutions still exist outside of Apple that optimize different parts of the testing process. You can find more information at `https://developer. apple.com/testflight/`.

Enterprise distribution does not require every device to be registered with Apple, but it must be delivered with MDM. Therefore, it is required to have direct access or some communication with the folks who manage the device, whether company-owned or otherwise. One point to keep in mind is that different MDM providers need different levels of involvement when they are asked to distribute apps on your behalf. They can make you shoot yourself in the foot, so to speak, by allowing a mismatch of the provisioning profile you would upload and the associated app bundle, resulting in an app with a pretty icon that won't launch. Other MDMs insist on direct interaction with your development team to reduce the possibility of issues. Keep in mind that certificates are an integral part of the process as well; therefore, they need to be renewed so that apps continue to function.

# Summary

In this chapter, we went over how apps are distributed and how they prove their integrity to the system once they are installed. We demonstrated the concept of locking a device into an app with **Guided Access**. Inter-app (and device) communication via extensions and **Continuity** was also discussed along with the new complimentary privacy controls for things like keyboards. As this chapter was about the customization and controls you'd want to place on apps, we gave a brief introduction to securely distributing your own in-house apps.

Since the time the iPhone first came along, the way many people interact with apps has changed significantly. Limited methods of installation, silos for categories of data and the capabilities of apps, and the keychain concept from OS X have all come to bear on iOS' overall security. You should now have enough background on how apps function to begin to understand why the limitations are the way they are, and what to keep in mind when you are tasked with securing app data.

In the next chapter, we will cover how iOS takes advantage of its hardware to create a secure environment even before we get to run any apps, starting from the moment the device is turned on.

# 3
# Encrypting Devices

In this chapter, we will be looking at iOS device encryption. You might think this would be the shortest chapter, as the filesystem itself has been fully encrypted for many revisions of the OS. This makes wiping the device when giving it away or selling it a very quick process, as all you're doing in essence is forgetting the master encryption key to unlock the already scrambled data and rendering it irretrievable. Wear leveling concerns for flash storage like those which are used in mobile devices nowadays makes this practical for another reason, as scrubbing all blocks (or pages) on the storage device is not necessary to ensure that the data is unrecoverable. We'll look into more topics than just the data bits at rest though, including network traffic and VPN.

While it may seem consumer-focused, we can now use these devices along with NFC (short for Near Field Communication) for payments, and concerns over employer liability for identity theft on a company-owned device can raise serious concerns. Security professionals must be even more in touch with what their company's policies are on protecting the company's best interests, while still allowing end users to be productive and enjoy full use of the "perk" that an iOS device might provide. Luckily many aspects of the iOS security model allow us to let the device roam untethered, and we can inform the end user how much data their device exposes when it is used normally and for everything a policy doesn't cover. Privacy also comes into play, so we'll touch on that as well.

To break it down, we'll discuss the following topics in this chapter:

- Revisiting OS initialization
- Passbook and Touch ID for Apple Pay
- Introduction to iOS network communication
- Privacy concerns with the Health App, HIPAA, and diagnostics
- Configuration Profile Encryption

# Secure boot and activating iOS

In a concept not unlike that of how Chrome OS ensures both the integrity of its firmware and that its kernel hasn't been tampered with, field upgrades can similarly proceed in a secured fashion with a feature called **verified boot.** When an iOS device starts up, it verifies the kernel and the rest of the read-only OS partition to confirm that it matches a particular signature. The process would be halted and the device would go back to Device Firmware Upgrade mode or DFU (which would also be accompanied by the **'Connect to iTunes'** screen) if the main OS partition is found to be nonfunctional. This can also be initiated if a wipe and reinstall is interrupted when initiated by iTunes, Apple Configurator, or the user themselves by going into the **General** section of **Settings** and navigating to **Reset | Erase All Content and Settings**.

The process from the time you power on the device to when you land in user space is referred to as the **secure boot chain**. A low-level bootloader performs verification to confirm whether the OS partition has not been tampered with, and as a whole, whether it has been signed by Apple. It uses on-board keys (which includes a root key, device-specific key, and group key to establish the chain of trust for cryptographic operations) that are included in the factory at time of manufacture. This low-level bootloader process finishes, and then, the iBoot process starts, which in turn starts the OS kernel.

On cellular devices that include the A7 or greater AMD architecture processor (which is in use in devices since the iPhone 5s), there is a region on the CPU that is responsible for cryptographic operations and this is referred to in marketing as the **Secure Enclave**. While it is not physically distinct, the highest importance is placed on making its functionality logically walled off from the processor's main function. The Secure Enclave interacts with the boot process by being called upon to start the cellular baseband through a separate but similar sequence, which is also responsible for checking the system software authorization.

Specifically, upon reactivation that is initiated by a manual erase or an OS restore, a validation process referred to as **System Software Authorization** is performed, which requires Internet access. A computer running iTunes or Apple Configurator can provide that conduit, or since iOS 5 and its PC Free features came along, you can connect to a Wi-Fi or cellular network to activate the device. As documented by Apple for some time in its iOS Security – White Paper, there is a specific, cryptographically secured process through which an individual device identifies itself to Apple while requesting activation to continue. Since Apple is the clearinghouse through which devices are allowed to run a specific OS version, previous OSes with any known security flaws are disallowed from being reapplied to an upgraded device that is capable of running it.

As we'll discuss in the next chapter, restoring a backup can skip this activation step on supervised devices, but that is a concern separate from the OS itself. A device running an older iOS version can therefore be erased without upgrading it, assuming that it has not been tampered with to fail verification.

Note that when an activation is required after an iOS installation on a cellular-capable device, a SIM card must be present. Apple uses this to generate a valid ECID to identify the device, so even when the device is prepared with iTunes or Apple Configurator but has no SIM card, this will result in an error and cause it to fail.

One may ask, of the many devices still being sold by Apple with the older processor architecture, how does it perform the cryptographic operations that are necessary to function? While this was not previously outlined by Apple, a common technique that is used is to gather entropy (or unpredictable results) from the many sensors on the device such as its gyroscope, accelerometer, or compass. The need for random numbers is obvious to anyone who is trying to make a secure system, since many implementations of a key generation process start by getting something distinct and sufficiently random to base its identity on.

# Passbook and Touch ID for Apple Pay

We briefly touched on **Touch ID** in *Chapter 1, iOS Security Overview*, but more implementation details around timeouts and other key-related interactions are better describe Apple's own iOS Security – White Paper (as they go to great lengths to make things as understandable as possible). At the time of writing, the most recent PDF was from October 2014 and it can be found at `https://www.apple.com/privacy/docs/iOS_Security_Guide_Oct_2014.pdf`.

As Touch ID should still just be considered an added convenience, sufficiently complex passcodes are, as always, recommended in all things that are security-related.

If your customers or users are like ours, they will forget their devices' passcodes after getting used to using Touch ID. Therefore, make sure that you do not leave your customers in a situation without MDM management (or backups, if your organization encourages it), especially if the ActiveSync-based "failed password attempt" limit is configured. Once the threshold is reached, it will cause their device to be wiped. This happens without adequate time to get assistance more often than we would like.

In the White Paper mentioned earlier, the importance and utility of the Secure Enclave is detailed. It may have come into existence in part to make the Touch ID fingerprint functionality as quick and seamless as possible, so that there would be no bottleneck for the required computation. One may think from Apple's marketing of the Secure Enclave that it is dedicated hardware, but just like the jailing of parts of the filesystem, this is mostly implemented as a technique to ensure that the software operations are wholly distinct and cannot run in the same memory or processor space when carrying out its functions.

How does this relate to Passbook? And how does a feature that most folks use for plane tickets (if ever) come into a discussion about security? Well, as we discussed previously, identity theft on a company-owned device could affect the company that provides the device to the employee, as evidenced by network equipment and mail systems that detect dangerous behavior like social security numbers being sent in plain text e-mail correspondence. With its early popularity and probable success of, Apple Pay, which is Apple's solution for NFC-based payments akin to Google Wallet, became an attractive target. Since Passbook is where Apple Pay stores the details of its credit and debit cards, securing it is important. Luckily, there are a few allowed vectors to get into Passbook, including the much-maligned QR code, and even then, there is limited functionality once a pass is installed.

The Passbook application has a built-in scanner that you can access by tapping on Scan Code from its splash screen, or by tapping the plus button in the top-right corner (if there's only one pass; otherwise, you'll see the plus button at the top, and it can be scrolled when in the list view). This is the same process through which you would add payment cards. For security reasons, neither addition stores the image to the Camera Roll on the device.

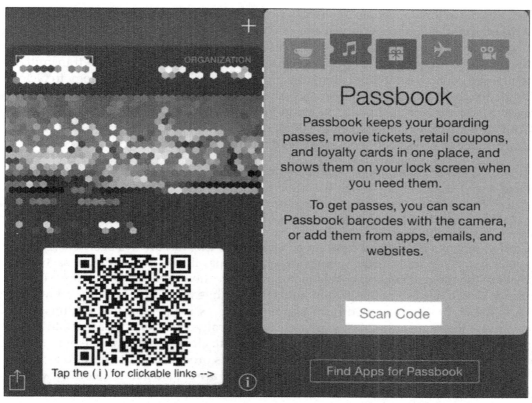

A Passbook pass and one process by which passes or cards can be added

Among other restrictions, you cannot, for instance, have an active hyperlink on the front of a pass. You can, however, send a notification to a device with the pass installed, and push updates to the pass so that it will dynamically change its content. Passbook passes with an active state (such as the lead up to boarding a plane) can be accessed when the device is locked, but updates to it can optionally be disabled in the pass itself, or both access to and notifications for Passbook can be disabled in the Touch ID and Passcode section of the Settings app or via a management system, along the lines of the restrictions that we'll demonstrate in *Chapter 5, Mobile Device Management.*

The attack vectors for Apple Pay haven't been exercised to the point that any working proof-of-concepts have been disclosed, but another quirk is that a pass can respond to location information. This could trigger a push notification when it is in the proximity of an iBeacon, Apple's branding for Bluetooth low energy transmitters, which can achieve something along the lines of a supplemental technology to GPS. While iBeacons themselves don't collect any information, Passbook will continue to evolve as an area of the phone to remain interested in. Neither NFC-based Apple Pay nor Passbook is yet available on the iPad; however, in-app or browser-based Apple Pay purchases work with the newest iPad hardware that has Touch ID.

Finally, one other note about purchases on the device is that when checking out from a web store, it may (when the site is a valid HTTPS one and certain fields are detected within the form) trigger a prompt to use the camera to take a picture of the card that you'd like to make the purchase with and fill in the detected information.

Card payment systems and fraud in general in the U.S. has always been a sore spot when compared to other countries, in particular things like ATM transactions that are the poorest version of two-factor authentication: something you have (the physical **card**) and something you know (**PIN**). While it's not particularly relevant to us as we are not as concerned from a payment processing perspective, but this seems to require the same amount of vigilance. Theoretically, one could take a photo of someone else's card, and through a coordinated attack involving social engineering, use it to authorize purchases. Apple can police this process, but as many concerns as there are about identity theft in general, there will always be that tradeoff between ease of use and protecting the system from abuse.

# Introduction to iOS network communication

We discussed Safari and the predictive search features that are enabled by default as the most obvious network traffic, besides e-mail and applications like Twitter and Facebook that can be accessed from more places on the device due to having account information built into the OS. Weather, Stocks, and Siri's data providers, are also allowed to use the network by default although you can disable just cellular access granularly. Speaking of which, depending on the carrier, swapping SIM cards (if the slot is unlocked on that particular cellular-capable iOS model) can be used to supplant international roaming plans by providing a number that is local to that place, or even just the data service as desired.

Besides this grab bag of overarching, networking-related concerns, we'll zoom in on Airdrop using wired connections on iOS, VPN, proxying, and filtering.

# AirDrop

A peer-to-peer way to share files on demand over an ad hoc Wi-Fi network with little or no setup has been present in the Mac OS for some time and it was added to iOS 7. **AirDrop** is this feature's branding and it now does the initial detection of nearby devices based on Bluetooth proximity and identifies information with Apple, again as the backend clearinghouse through which Apple ID identities are processed. This adds anonymity to the process of checking whether we know the person to whom we are sending the file, and can populate the round icon representing the other device with the contact's locally assigned image.

As of iOS 8 and OS X 10.10, Yosemite, computers can also perform this handshake and transfer of data. Due to its ease of use and lack of authentication before allowing the sending end to transmit (among other reasons), many IT departments disabled the early implementations of AirDrop on the Mac. Multicast traffic is less of a network-related concern when it is peer-to-peer and restricted to Wi-Fi, but identity verification with its associated metadata among many other cryptographic processes that do hit the network, requires a significant amount of trust in Apple.

**Note** that this is one of the bigger issues that people with privacy and security concerns express about vendors who have made choices similar to Apple. This is also commonly discussed in relation to their iMessage service; part of the condition of using the service is that you must implicitly trust that Apple is properly securing and restricting access to the keys that the participants use.

Depending on the type of file that is being transferred, compatible applications are displayed on the receiving end to then take action. The following screenshot shows a device that has received a file over AirDrop:

Options presented when a ringtone is received over AirDrop

# A bug or a feature?

We long ago made the assertion that Apple cheats by being able to synchronize its software with its own hardware. Another maxim of Apple IT is that in general, Apple doesn't care about the developer community, Apple doesn't care about us. Their priorities could reasonably be arranged as follows:

- The customers
- Themselves and their side of the overlap between partners and their platforms
- Lastly, anybody else who would wish them well along the way to improve the experience of the first two

This is not new, nor should anyone expect them to change in the light of their success. However, they sometimes make it easier for all the parties involved by having an extensively shared code base between iOS devices. This includes another product, the **Apple TV**, which is often overlooked or discarded as not a serious endeavor, but which we in IT get a surprise benefit: it includes Ethernet drivers to support its hardware, which in turn is present across all iOS installations ever since its smaller, hockey puck form factor was introduced.

An *unintentional* bit of functionality that we gain from this is through a technique that involves the following things:

- A powered USB hub
- The Lightning to USB Camera Adapter (intended to connect a camera with an iOS device to import photos into iPhoto or other iOS applications)
- An Apple USB Ethernet Adapter

By connecting the Lightning to USB Camera Adapter to the upstream port of the USB hub and the Ethernet Adapter in any downstream port, a device should be able to use this configuration to get on the wired network. While this part of the networking stack doesn't seem particularly optimized, forensic capture through more traditional means (mirroring ports, and so on) is possible without the involvement of any computer. (We will, however, cover Apple's supported processes to accomplish iOS packet tracing in *Chapter 6, Debugging and Conclusion*.) An illustration of this setup is documented in terms of passcode removal via MDM at `https://www.afp548.com/2014/05/07/mdm-passcode-removal-from-an-offline-ios-device/`.

Common human input devices such as barcode scanners or keyboards can be used with the Lightning to USB Camera Adapter for ease of input and they are a great way to prevent folks from having to use their thumbs for data entry en masse. While the iOS device may bark that the accessory is not supported, you may add a hidden functionality and significantly streamline interactions if all the hardware is compliant and it all goes well.

# VPN (Always-On, APN, Per-App, On-Demand)

Since very early on, you have been able to configure and initiate a VPN connection in the **Settings** of an iOS device, which started with the more prevalent gateways in use (including flavors of Cisco IPSec, and the raccoon-based L2TP or PPTP projects which OS X Server relies on). Now, there are more ways to tunnel traffic than you can figuratively shake a metaphorical stick at. As the demand to enable more functionality on iOS is ever increasing, Apple has added support for RSA SecurID two-factor tokens in the built-in configuration settings as well.

As with other complex settings, you could also use a configuration profile to simplify the setup for end users, which we will touch on in *Chapter 5, Mobile Device Management*.

A newer feature, also available for use when configured with a profile or manually, is the ability to lock the device into tunneling all its traffic through a VPN tunnel with an **AlwaysOn** configuration. This is exposed to end users with a **Send All Traffic** slider when optional. For it to be managed so that it is locked into the **ON** position, the appropriate configuration profile needs to be in place and the device needs to be in a state called **Supervision**, which we will describe in detail in the next chapter.

The following screenshot shows a VPN connection, with options for **RSA SecurID**, **Send All Traffic**, and so on:

A VPN connection with options for RSA SecurID tokens and Send All Traffic

An older, more obscure method of securing data service access with the cooperation of your cellular provider is via an **Access Point Name** configuration, but it's not something that the authors of this book come across very often any more in the real world. You may forgive the comparison of APN to an extension of the corporate LAN, although with the popularity and toolset around VPNs becoming so commonplace, it's understandable that this cellular-only technique would fall by the wayside.

When paired with proper certificates and a configuration profile to define the domains that require a VPN connection, **VPN On Demand** enables on-the-fly connections to be made when a device tries to connect to a given domain. Many elaborate checks are also possible on a network state change, including SSID, reachable server detection, and DNS server settings so that **On Demand** can be turned off when it's 'on-network'. This is especially useful in split-domain DNS configurations.

**Per-App** is by far the most attractive app, as when an organization has provided an app they commonly also want to secure all the traffic that the app will generate. As always, however, the devil is in the details. A few VPN gateways and fewer apps are set to enable this behavior. Organizations may find any of the more advanced implementations tricky, as you need a more sophisticated gateway setup with compatible hardware and software, which can also require significant preparation from a certificate infrastructure perspective.

The most simple and possibly hardest to manage are the specific apps on the App Store from VPN gateway vendors, some of which merely embed a web browser that allows you to connect to sites on a remote network once the connection is established.

Otherwise, you can just build all your workflows into an app such as Good, enables or wrap them into a container app that does all the network traffic and business interactions for you. Even more attractive is securing the transport and data at rest when interacting with your organization's applications and sidestepping all of this tomfoolery. Conjure to mind the meme of the character Boromir from The Lord of the Rings saying that *one does not simply walk into Mordor*, the twist being that one does not simply trust any client accessing your data to be properly secured even if they have provided valid credentials. But we can only go so crazy until it becomes prohibitive to restrict access that folks need to do their jobs.

# Global HTTP Proxy, caching, and the web content filter

Due to concerns over and regulation of the network traffic of iOS devices in school environments, Apple started with a Global HTTP Proxy feature to enable the caching and proxying of traffic, with the additional benefit of working off-campus and on cellular devices. Vendors that specialize in ensuring the uptime of the service's gateway are important to partner with, and commonly network security appliances have taken on this role among their other services. As this is only HTTP, it doesn't address many mandated regulations for protecting students in certain jurisdictions, but it was a start at alleviating some network inspection and caching needs.

Apple included a Caching Service in the 2.2 release of its Server application, which is distributed as an add-on to regular OS X. You can set this up and cache content for a NAT's local network in order to improve performance during OS updates or when other frequently accessed data is requested by many devices. We do not get many features with this solution though, as you cannot poison the cache to ensure that certain applications or content are made unavailable on your network. Some have resorted to hijacking DNS requests on port 80 to `mesu.apple.com`, for example, so that OS updates cannot take place while on-network. Other content that is enabled by default with this service is iTunes, iOS App Store, Mac App Store, and iBooks Store purchases along with Mac and iOS Updates.

This is all, of course, only HTTP and it is more about relieving network load than limiting the type of content that is accessible on the devices. Only recently did Apple add the ability to subscribe to content filter updates for HTTPS sites, or granularly whitelist or blacklist sites. As discussed earlier, a reliable partner who understands your organization's policies is critical to implement a filter that doesn't become a hindrance or a block to your customers' productivity.

As discussed with the locking of **AlwaysOn** VPN settings, devices must be in the supervised state to use either Global HTTP Proxy or the web content filter. (This makes sense as a supervised device can have settings locked that end users cannot disable at will.)

# Privacy-related concerns

Just as earlier when we discussed Apple Pay, you may find it odd to see a section on privacy, but as we said, these days with identity theft and other ways customers can leak data through social engineering, the concerns for organizations are more pressing. Practically speaking, it's just a lot of overhead when directory harvest attacks catch the less-astute employees who fall for tricks that cause them to hand over their credentials, and then administrators need to go through the process of locking them out and fixing their mailboxes.

Administrative overhead is the least of the concerns for larger, well-known internet companies that would be very embarrassed, at the very least, if their employees were phished or were clumsy with their credentials. It became public that one company in particular had deployed a plug-in to the web browser that they developed whose purpose was to detect when network credentials were being entered in an insecure or bogus form, thereby effectively preventing that method of exposure. The Mac admin community gets a lot of their ideas and best practices from this company, which rhymes with "froogle".

Just as there are regulations around processing credit cards — the most commonly known is PCI (short for the Payment Card Industry) Security Standards Council — there are healthcare industry standards around privacy which are included as part of HIPAA (or the Health Insurance Portability and Accountability Act). Part of this statute classifies certain pieces of health-related information to be protected, which includes a surprisingly broad range of data — even something as simple as names, when attached to data in a particular context become sensitive and important to control access to.

We'll cover two examples of new ways the data is collected on iOS devices (and the iPhone in particular) to demonstrate how this is a constantly evolving topic that requires appropriate attention based on your dealings with the healthcare industry. Even colleges are trying to reduce the risk of lawsuits due to information in student records getting into the wrong hands, so hopefully you can work with the policymakers at your institution to craft appropriate policies.

# Lesser-known ways for Apple to gather diagnostics

First, you may not realize how easy it is for Apple to be invited into the goings-on of their devices. Just recently we came across an iOS device that needed to be serviced. If you go to Apple's site and say that you would like to set up a Genius Bar, in-store technical support appointment, they can prompt you to send in identification and diagnostic data right there on the spot (presumably to deliver a better, more efficient experience). Further, to prove ownership over the phone, Apple can send a push notification with a PIN to a device logged into the iCloud account if you provide other identification information about the device.

Now, in the scenario that we just described for collecting identification and diagnostic data, you may think that there would be a high bar to have access to the mechanism that collects this data. However, there are self-servicing organization statuses that can be granted to large companies and institutions that do not want to get service through third-party service providers or the Apple Store's Genius Bar. While improving the repair experience for the customers of an organization, the devices that diagnostics can be run on are not, to our knowledge, limited to the ones purchased by the organization.

One would think the binding agreements placed on those with access to self-service organization status through a service provided by Apple called **Global Service Exchange** would prevent foul play. Through conversations with those who do have access to these diagnostics, we can report that there are little differences in what can be seen in diagnostic logs on the device. This service has a bit more hardware repair-related information that would be helpful for participating in recall or warranty upgrade programs that Apple is forced to do from time to time. For example, in the case of certain models of iPhone 5, there was a known issue where the home button lost functionality after being in use for a certain period of time, which was therefore made eligible for exchange.

As we will drive home in *Chapter 6, Debugging and Conclusion* regarding the attack vectors a device is exposed to once pairing to a computer is allowed, one may consider this an acceptable trade-off for a better experience when the average consumer needs their device fixed. The data gathered and collectable is limited, but Apple will continue to dance this line between things like not showing their third-party developers much in the way of feedback from customers, to preventing too much exposure like the well-publicized deletion of the devices of a prominent journalist for Wired whose iCloud account was hacked into.

# Health app

Another class of data that many would consider private is their activity. iOS 8 introduced frameworks to help the various healthcare companies that develop hardware accessories to interact with health data.

Glaringly missing at launch, however, was a class of period tracking data for women. As third-party iOS apps have been built to track this from the beginning of the existence of the App Store, with recent standouts covering narrowly-targeted tasks relating to breastfeeding, this is rather odd. Developers couldn't even submit apps leveraging the framework until several revisions of iOS 8, and still, Nike Fuel is a notable third-party that is able to leverage its data with a named inclusion in the Health app.

As of the launch of the iPhone 5s, a sensor which functions as a pedometer is included in all iPhones. Apple's marketing team branded the hardware that manages the caching and processing of health sensor-specific data the M7 motion coprocessor, with version numbering in sync with its in-house ARM line of processors, which is currently A8. This removes the need for as many external sensors on devices, like those left out of the design of the Apple Watch (that was proposed at the time of writing). Additionally, as of the Health app bundled with iOS 8, step and running data is tracked and displayed by default, whether you explicitly enable it or not.

You can see this combination of GPS and accelerometer sensors in action for yourself by noticing the step data logged in the Health app without any opt-in on your part. There are, in fact, no settings for the app whatsoever. Only privacy settings can be managed to disallow apps that have requested access to the warehouse of data stored within, whether the phone's own sensors logged it or an accessory was the original source. In the following screenshot, you will get to see automatically logged step and distance data:

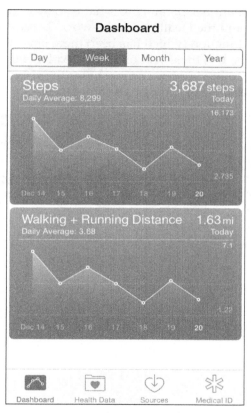

Automatically logged step and distance data

One other thing that you can interact with could be a potential source of information leakage, but is implemented as an opt-in feature: an "in case of emergency" function.

A story from a popular site by Dave Pell titled 'My Head is in the Cloud' recounts how his babysitter doesn't have her boyfriend's cell phone number memorized, and when she was injured and her cell phone was wrecked, they had no way to contact him. It's as if this feature was designed with this scenario (minus the destroyed phone) in mind.

You can add your information separately to what is then accessible by apps that tie into the Health app (and the HealthKit framework therein) so that from the lock screen's emergency call function (which has been there since the first iPhone, as federally mandated in the US) there will be a new text label in the lower left-hand corner: Medical ID. The following screenshot shows the screen that shows the information to aid first responders in case of emergencies:

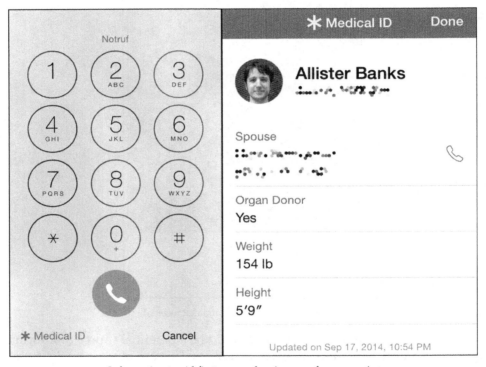

Information to aid first responders in case of emergencies

This tells some vital statistics, and most importantly, in case the phone's owner is unable to communicate, whom to contact (or to be completely maudlin, the next of kin) with a handy call button next to it so that they are more likely to pick up the call.

# Configuration profiles

If you have any familiarity with how OS X stores its configuration files, it would not be too much of a surprise to hear that a profile that was implemented for iOS management is also a specific flavor of XML. Instead of a central registry like you have on Windows, there's different, often granularly set files or (often sqlite3) databases with which an application or the operating environment itself is customized. However, this is not as important as the framework with which changes are enforced on the system, and so, a trip back to OS X would actually be useful, as that was what inspired much of the architecture of iOS.

Without management, changes can still be applied by touching key-value pairs in these XML files in what are called **preference domains**. The files themselves are referred to as property lists and carry the `.plist` file extension. A common binary used to interact with these `.plist` files at the command line is the defaults command, although system frameworks are exposed to scripting languages to directly interact with the underlying API.

As with a traditional directory service, however, settings can be inherited from a network-based central database, the payload for which on Windows is commonly group policy objects or GPOs. Macs have a framework that is referred to as Managed Client for OS X or MCX. By applying MCX settings to a computer or computer group, they would all have the same settings enforced no matter who used the device, but user or group-level settings would depend upon who's logged in. Just as with non-network aware preference domains, MCX-enforced property list files are stored near the local user and group database on the filesystem, where it is cached to maintain the settings off network. Admin users could optionally override any settings when logging in, for quick troubleshooting of configurations.

Instead of MCX as the delivery method, profiles came to the Mac as an additional way to manage settings in OS X 10.7 and became more powerful; now, a configuration profile can affect changes that MCX had not previously been able to such as networking-related settings among others. The idea was to go back to the Mac and allow management systems to use the same format, XML files with the `mobileconfig` extension, in many cases applying the same settings. So, to recap, configurations can be set on the Mac through the following ways:

- Simple `.plist` files residing at the same location where they'd be found in a default installation and can be interacted with via the defaults command

- The `.plist` files with specific MCX stanzas, which was the previous way in which you could implement management from a central user/group/ computer database like LDAP

- Configuration profiles, which is the newer, cross-platform (between iOS and Mac) method of applying management settings

With configuration profiles, just like MCX, you can group computers and users or manage them individually. As we will demonstrate in *Chapter 5, Mobile Device Management*, the terminology used with the Server application's **Profile Manager** service is to use a device to refer to an iOS device or a Mac, and you can even inherit users and groups from Active Directory. The device level of management within a profile is called the **System scope**, whereas anything that would apply granularly to a **User** is called just that. The following screenshot shows an example of an Apple-flavored XML file, with the System Payload scope, which means that it will take effect device-wide, instead of being scoped to a particular user:

```xml
<?xml version="1.0" encoding="UTF-8"?>
<!DOCTYPE plist PUBLIC "-//Apple//DTD PLIST 1.0//EN" "http://www.apple.com/DTDs/PropertyList-1.0.dtd">
<plist version="1.0">
 <dict>
    <key>PayloadIdentifier</key>
    <string>com.apple.mdm.host.example.com.0499212E-330E-479F-825A-D08AE9DAFD4C.alacarte</string>
    <key>PayloadRemovalDisallowed</key>
    <false/>
    <key>PayloadScope</key>
    <string>System</string>
    <key>PayloadType</key>
    <string>Configuration</string>
    <key>PayloadUUID</key>
    <string>0499212E-330E-479F-825A-D08AE9DAFD4C</string>
    <key>PayloadOrganization</key>
    <string>Example Org</string>
    <key>PayloadVersion</key>
    <integer>1</integer>
    <key>PayloadDisplayName</key>
    <string>Settings for radius-withcert</string>
    <key>PayloadContent</key>
    <array>
      <dict>
        <key>PayloadType</key>
        <string>com.apple.security.pkcs1</string>
```

An example of an Apple-flavored XML file, with the System Payload scope, meaning it is to take effect device-wide instead of being scoped to a particular user

Notice that the DOCTYPE in the preceding screenshot specifically calls out Apple, and settings are structured with no particular ordering since it has a hash or dict (short for dictionary) as the base type. The following screenshot has more details on this 802.1x-specific configuration:

```
<key>EAPClientConfiguration</key>
<dict>
    <key>AcceptEAPTypes</key>
    <array>█</array>
    <key>OneTimeUserPassword</key>
    <false/>
    <key>PayloadCertificateAnchorUUID</key>
    <array>█</array>
    <key>UserName</key>
    <string/>
    <key>SystemModeCredentialsSource</key>
    <string>ActiveDirectory</string>
    <key>UserPassword</key>
    <string/>
    <key>TTLSInnerAuthentication</key>
    <string>MSCHAPv2</string>
</dict>
<key>ProxyType</key>
<string>None</string>
<key>AuthenticationMethod</key>
<string>directory</string>
<key>Interface</key>
<string>BuiltInWireless</string>
<key>HIDDEN_NETWORK</key>
<true/>
<key>SSID_STR</key>
<string>radiuswifi</string>
```

A Wi-Fi configuration profile, which would tell the radius controller that Active Directory credentials will be used for 802.1x authentication

There is, however, no concept of binding an iOS device to a directory service, nor of different users having customized settings, whereas Macs can take both into account. Products even exist to manage settings for Macs within the same interface as GPO for PCs. For iOS though, the MDM service itself needs to be aware of the groupings and management settings which it can then act upon to hand down configurations to devices. This is in contrast to Macs, which can even be told to provide authentication to radius controllers over Wi-Fi with Active Directory credentials at the login window, as shown in the preceding screenshot. If you deployed the profile pictured previously to an iOS device, it may very well ignore the unused options or fail altogether.

Now that we have seen more about the format and how it's scoped to devices, let's look into the history of this management format. Apple's canonical reference of an interface with which to construct the settings available for managing iOS devices first appeared in a tool for Windows and Mac called **iPhone Configuration Utility** (or **iPCU** for short, which makes it sound like one of those places you can get an associate's degree on the internet). It was originally released back when the OS was called iPhone OS 2. (Really, it was OS/2 Warp. Now that was an OS!) When constructing a configuration profile, you would see management options grouped into sections in a sidebar on the left, and you would interact with various fields on the right. The following screenshot shows the configuration profile creation/editing in the iPCU interface:

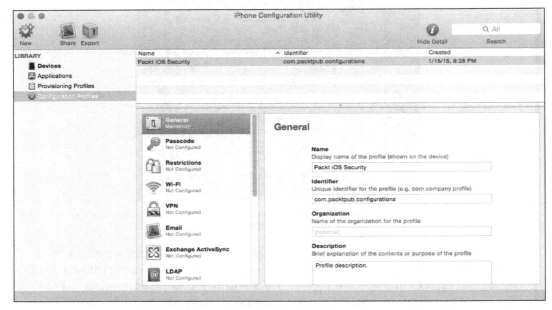

Configuration profile creation/editing in the iPCU interface

You could even view logs (unlike the mere diagnostic reports we did earlier), which came in handy while you applied a profile to see where things went off the track when a configuration wasn't valid. The following screenshot shows the logged output (essentially syslog output in a console running on the device) displayed while applying a profile:

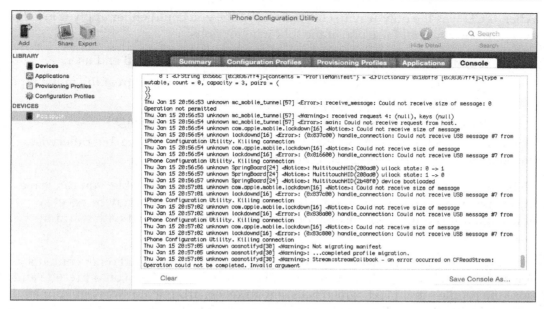

Logged output (essentially syslog output in a console running on the device) displayed while applying a profile

iPCU has been discontinued. It can no longer view logs on iOS 8 devices and it is no longer available to download for Windows or Mac. This is probably a good thing as it hadn't been updated since iOS 6. It launched the interface paradigm for many configuration profile interfaces and no Apple tool has yet replaced the ease-of-use of its console feature. See *Chapter 6, Debugging and Conclusion*, for details on `libimobiledevice`, which may have a similar functionality.

> For essentially opening a console on an iOS device and viewing logs (as long as the device has been paired), one of our excellent technical reviewers, Jeremy Agostino, recommends iOS Console, which is available at `http://lemonjar.com/iosconsole`.

# Signing, encryption, and delivery

When a properly configured and secure MDM pushes a configuration profile to a device, it will be signed as any piece of code should be that wants to prove its identity and be trusted by devices. It should also encrypt its payload to protect any sensitive data contained within. However, the usual delivery method, pulled over-the-air by the device once told to check in by Apple's Push Notification Service, is not the only transport mechanism.

When iPCU was the only way to construct a profile, you could either apply it locally over USB, or you could use one of the following options:

- E-mail it to each applicable device by way of the associated end user
- Put it on a properly configured web server (which would treat the mime type accordingly for access from mobile safari on devices)
- Send it by a text message (remember, this predated iMessage)

Now, there are a few other tools that can apply a profile to a device, but otherwise, the non-MDM delivery mechanisms are unchanged.

To break down the format of configuration profiles that are available, you can leave the profile in plain text with no signature and edit it at will. This may be rejected or just not applied if folks refuse to continue after being presented with warning prompts when asked to install it.

You could sign but not encrypt the profile, leaving the payload and other contents able to be inspected in plain text. A barely recognizable text blob would precede and close the profile's main text, which is its signature, ensuring that it was not tampered with. If it was altered after signing, any subsequent installations would be refused.

Finally, the entire profile could be encrypted, making it rely on a working, compatible PKI relationship that is normally based on a Remote Management profile being installed on the device, which an MDM service would put on at enrollment time.

 Configuration profile signatures use the **Cryptographic Message Syntax (CMS)** standard. While not exactly simple, one could use openssl on various operating systems in tandem with a root certificate from a trusted certificate authority to apply signatures to configuration profiles, which devices will then see as trusted.

# Summary

This chapter was a bit of a grab bag of the more fundamental concepts of how the device handles encryption. Instead of being a complete derivative of Apple's iOS Security White Paper, we presented the newer quirks and real-world application of some of the topics around encrypting the main functions of the device. We discussed how the system is prepared at the factory with security in mind through its secure boot process. The addition of NFC payments via Apple Pay led us to investigate Passbook and its integration with Touch ID. Networking-related concerns like VPN, AirDrop, Proxies, and Filters were also discussed along with a way of utilizing a wired network connection. The Health app and Medical ID were toured briefly. Finally, we prepared for applying management by detailing what the actual files and formats are that manage settings on both iOS and Mac.

**Bring Your Own Device (BYOD)** programs often overlap with how regular consumers want to use what is, in fact, their device. While keeping that in mind, as professionals we need to balance control over our data with taking full advantage of the utility of the device. Hopefully, this also gets you thinking about privacy as a topic that goes hand-in-hand with security, and lays the groundwork for the application of management settings to bring about productivity in employees, which we'll be covering over the next two chapters.

# 4
# Organizational Controls

Now, we'll move on to explore the concepts involved in managing iOS devices from a central location on-premises. This includes device supervision, Activation Lock, Single App Mode, and more basic options presented by the old stalwart, ActiveSync. For most of the time, we will be looking at a tool called **Apple Configurator** that is developed by Apple. We consider it to be one of the easiest tools to recommend for environments that need more hands-on control when officially supporting iOS, either when migrating to a **BYOD** (short form for bring your own device) environment or in conjunction with an MDM. It fits a couple of specific workflows very well and has some features that are vital for hardening devices.

Besides Apple Configurator, which at the very least can provide a good reference for showing Apple's acknowledged use cases for starting with device management, we will also introduce Apple's Device Enrollment Program or DEP. Activation Lock is a thornier topic now, so we'll touch on this as well. Just to transition from **Guided Access**, which was covered in *Chapter 2, Introducing App Security*, we'll also discuss App Lock when we explain the difference between it interacting with **Guided Access** and Single App Mode. And, before we get into full-blown MDM in the following chapter, we will discuss ActiveSync as one of the original over-the-air management frameworks.

In brief, this chapter's topics are as follows:

- Apple Configurator
- Preparation, supervision, and assignment of iOS devices
- The distribution of apps with Apple Configurator and the Volume Purchase Program
- Activation Lock and Find My iPhone
- The Device Enrollment Program versus Apple Configurator
- App Lock and Single App Mode in contrast to **Guided Access**
- Refresher on what ActiveSync provides on iOS

# Apple Configurator

Before the release of Apple Configurator on the Mac App Store, there were three other sanctioned applications for interaction with iOS devices: iTunes, Xcode, and **iPhone Configuration Utility (iPCU)**. Xcode had the capability to connect multiple devices simultaneously, but even that functionality was limited for running tests on devices or for restoring a version of iOS. Still, we were without any concept of efficient, directly connected management tools, nor even the hint of integration with a directory service.

When the iPad was released, it did not come with a manual like a lawn mower, which shows you what its intended usage is and how to sharpen the blades. Apple just about said the same thing to its customers that it says to its developers, something to the effect of "we can't wait to see what YOU do with it", as if it was still an open question as to what its most popular use would be. Apple products have, however, historically been used extensively in education and the price was commonly a half to a third of the least expensive laptop Mac. This led to an influx of iPads in environments that might not have been particularly prepared to have so many computing devices on Wi-Fi. This leads us back to the lack of applications that allow tethered preparation and maintenance of many devices at once.

Perhaps, if customers that used Apple products for educational purposes in particular were asked what they wanted, as the paraphrased saying attributed to Henry Ford goes, they would have said a faster horse; instead they got Apple Configurator. We do not want to be repetitive, but we must recall that Apple's priorities are its customers first and foremost, and they sell an astounding amount of products to regular consumers. One may be inclined to cut them, and companies like Amazon who are selling to the general public with success, some slack, which is hard. Amazon's not trying to be CDW and Apple can't be everything to everyone; (although it has never stopped the sprawl of iTunes, which the Apple TV Assistant built into Apple Configurator which has a faint whiff of.)

Back in *Chapter 2, Introducing App Security*, we mentioned about the **Volume Purchase Program** (**VPP**) that Apple offers. This was an integral part of what was considered going into designing Apple Configurator, along with the Supervision concept that we've been hinting at throughout the book so far. However, before we get into that, let's discuss workflows.

# Intended workflows

Of all the iOS form factors, at 9.6", the original and canonical iPad screen is comparably sized to 8.5" x 11" or an A4 sheet of paper, if you lose the margins and enjoyed staring at a light bulb all the time. (What? you don't *prefer* emissive screens?) If a telecom field worker has visited your home or business recently, you might have noticed that they now almost exclusively use tablets. Similarly, airlines have been giving their staff handheld devices for some time. When taking this rapid adoption of mobile devices into account, and recalling who Apple usually cares about when designing solutions, it may make more sense as to how Apple Configurator came into being.

An iPad can conceivably replace a utility worker's clipboard or a student's three-ring binders and streamline processes along the way. Airline pilots began demanding iPads to replace their ungainly and heavy binders of airport and route maps, which actually saved fuel due to the drop in weight. We can start to see that devices will be used in a multitude of ways, but a particularly apt case is high-service and quick-turnaround environments, loaded with the apps and data people need to get their work done.

Apple Configurator's release was groundbreaking in that it was a series of firsts:

- Applications could be handed out in bulk without MDM, *and these apps could then be reclaimed*

- Backups could be created and restored without iTunes *and restored or refreshed en masse*

- New, more locked-down restrictions could be enabled

Educational institutions segment time into classes and they often gather devices in labs or carts. Hospitals and utility workers have shifts and can make a station around a time clock or a gathering place for devices, from where they can be checked in and out from. It is widely reported that Apple does not have a colossal R&D footprint, so when they make a tool they have to please as many end users as possible. They don't have the resources to quality assure and develop features that can serve every market. Please keep all of this in mind as we discuss what Apple Configurator can do, with at least an understanding of why it doesn't make French fries four different ways.

The following screenshot shows the splash screen on starting Apple Configurator for the first time, which graphically introduces its three modes:

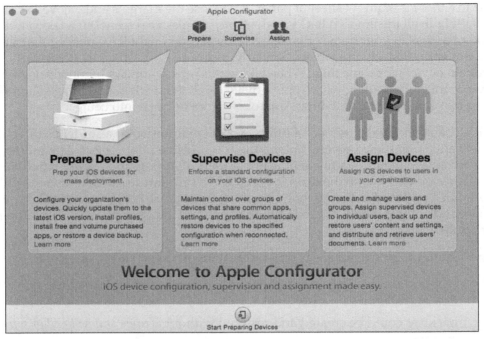

The splash screen on starting Apple Configurator for the first time graphically introduces its three modes

# The interaction modes – Prepare, Supervise, and Assign

After acquiring Apple Configurator from the Mac App Store (it is free, but requires a Mac at this time), you're greeted with an image that breaks down its three cumulative modes of operation. First, there are the capabilities of the Prepare mode, which are as follows:

- Naming the device (this includes the option of sequential, numeric naming if you are preparing multiple devices at once, as it can handle up to 30 devices concurrently)
- Creating a (unsupervised) backup

- Applying a software update (which caches that version) and optionally, wiping the device in the process
- Importing, creating, exporting and/or applying configuration profiles

Finally, flipping a switch to move the device to the next mode, *Supervision*

Flipping this switch to make the device become supervised changes the behavior of Apple Configurator's options. Therefore, you must then wipe the device and apply the most recent iOS update.

One might say that these distinctions help to prove that the device is indeed owned and under the control of the institution managing these devices, as it is assumed that regular people wouldn't let IT seize their property and remove all personalization or customization. (If they are like our customers at least.) However, Apple Configurator can easily be used in Prepare mode to lightly run an OS update, install a configuration profile, or even perform a backup and restoration.

 Our technical editor points out that the device must trust the computer running Apple Configurator first to even do these light tasks, as we'll exploit in *Chapter 6, Debugging and Conclusion*.

This helps us to clearly define the distinction between preparation and supervision, as the second layer's powerful functionality rests on top of the first. The last mode, Assign, has just two additions:

- First, you can leverage a local or network-based directory service
- Second, the data created by a user from the directory can be stored on the computer running Apple Configurator

This allows the user to check in or check out of data as well as sets of apps, and it can also aid in the distribution of documents to devices that have compatible apps installed on them. It may seem like we're jumping ahead to discuss the Assign mode, but that's really the only additional feature.

Other than that, as whiz-bang features go, if users from the directory service have images associated with their LDAP records, there is a preference to show these images on the lock screen when assigning devices. You will access it from the **Apple Configurator** menu in the top left-hand corner of the screen, under **Preferences**. However, the stars have never aligned to the point that we've seen that in use in the real world. The following screenshot shows, in **Preferences**, where an assigned device can be configured to use an image from LDAP:

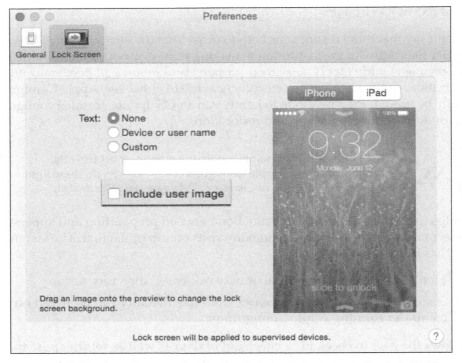

In **Preferences**, where an assigned device can be configured to use an image from LDAP

# The importance of supervision

Once the device has been wiped and updated by being tethered to a computer running Apple Configurator, you can take advantage of several options. These include:

- Customizing the lock screen image, as shown in the preceding image, optionally with the device's name or some other static text

- Enabling various network-related features including Always-On VPN, Content filters, Global HTTP proxy (as discussed in the previous chapter), and cellular data modifications

- Restricting various features such as the manual installation of configuration profiles, AirDrop, account modifications including Find My Friends, enabling other on-device restrictions, education-specific concerns like Siri's profanity filter, and whitelisting destinations or presetting passcodes for AirPlay

- Hide (by which we mean disable, to bring about the effect that the app is not shown) built-in applications like Game Center, iTunes Store, iMessage, Podcasts, or store components like In-App Purchase or the iBooks Store

- Stop the removal of any other apps, including the ones that Apple Configurator may have installed, or prevent the addition of any so-called Internet accounts (such as Facebook, Twitter, and so on) or e-mail accounts

 Restricting Safari does not require supervision, but it is a common error to believe that you'll allow all the web functionality you want by using a Web Clip payload in a configuration profile. For example, for accessing your intranet only. If you restrict Safari, the app will be removed and Web Clips will not even launch if present.

A bigger point than even these settings, which were advocated by so many of Apple's customers in large institutions, is the ability to install profiles with zero taps. If the device is still in Prepare mode, you'll need to respond to the prompts on the screen to accept certificate notifications, learn about what the profile will do to the device, and eventually, install, and then tap on done, per profile. Loading a profile onto a supervised device is silent. In fact, when restoring the backup to supervised devices, you don't even need to go through any setup or activation steps. (More recent versions of Apple Configurator can allow similar behavior without restoring a backup, by selecting which prompts to skip.)

If this wasn't a security book, we could probably stop here. However, by far the biggest point from a security perspective is the fact that, by default, a supervised device can be disabled from connecting to any other computer running Apple Configurator. An attacker cannot piggyback on iTunes to target another device too. This mitigates many of the pairing-based complications that we'll be discussing in *Chapter 6, Debugging and Conclusion*. In fact, if it was desirable to allow moving any content to the device from another computer, the device must be designated *at time of supervision* to **Allow devices to connect to other Macs** (by which they imply PCs as well).

Further, if a specific configuration profile with a restriction payload is applied, **Allow pairing with non-Configurator hosts** must also be selected. If you want to, this can allow you to optionally disable pairing later via MDM, in case it is not clear whether your end users will need it at the time of supervision, but if you are using Apple Configurator to supervise the device, then it must be connected to the computer again. You can see each of these settings in the following screenshot:

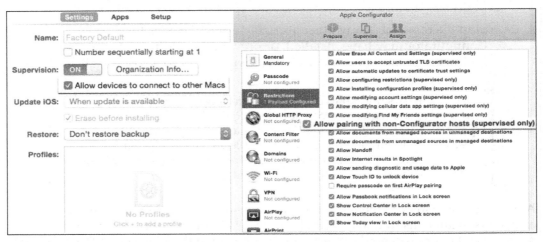

The two settings that must align for devices to be allowed to pair with any computer

When discussing workflows, we said Apple Configurator is a good fit for high-service, fast-turnaround use cases, which leads to another big feature of supervision: the ability to refresh the device to a stored state upon reconnection. If this includes the restoration of a larger backup with many apps, this can be a more lengthy process, but in any case, all of the ingredients are cached locally in Apple Configurator's support directories. (Apps such as iMovie and Keynote run in to hundreds of MBs and flash storage in general is optimized for reading and not writing, so it's good to measure if the cycle time meets your expectations.) This can essentially reimage the iOS device if Apple Configurator is open on the computer to which the device is attached.

Optionally, in the event you are not restoring a backup, you can also have apps and profiles that may have been added to the deleted device, so user training regarding supervised devices is very important. If this behavior is not desired for any reason, you must at least temporarily turn off these settings in Apple Configurator's Preferences, as shown in the following screenshot:

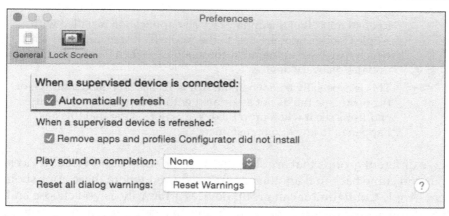

In **Preferences** where supervised devices are configured to automatically refresh when they are connected

# Apps, VPP, and Apple Configurator

When the usage model is one customer for one device, an MDM can prompt an end user for their Apple ID. Apple Configurator doesn't require a user that receives a device prepared by it to plug anything in, allowing shared usage models that just weren't possible before.

If an Apple ID is authorized for use on the computer running Apple Configurator, even if it is not associated with VPP, you can go ahead and import and distribute free applications. The recommended way to go about obtaining the .ipa files (the archived bundles that are iOS applications, as discussed in *Chapter 2, Introducing App Security*) is to download them from the App Store section in iTunes. However, no matter what ID the app was downloaded with (for example, if an iOS device already synched with the computer and backed up its purchases with iTunes), the DRM can be removed from the app bundle and imported with whatever Apple ID Apple Configurator wants to use. However, if you forget to authorize the computer in iTunes, you'd see the following error:

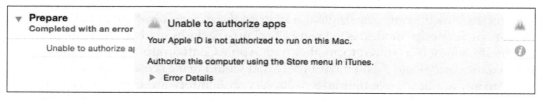

When an app to be installed on a device is imported without the associated Apple ID authorized in iTunes

Keep in mind that the updates for any application installed with Apple Configurator are tied to the Apple ID it was imported with, which may have unintended consequences when it prompts for updates on every device.

This is especially true when the Apple ID has an e-mail address for the username that is not associated with your institution, because end users see it when prompted. We're not saying that this has happened to any of our customers.

If you have different groups that are sharing the same set of supervised devices, apps can go out and come back in if another setup is required where these apps shouldn't be present. Apple Configurator can group devices arbitrarily as you choose and apply settings as needed, and apps are one of the things that can come along for the ride.

These processes are just the same for paid apps that have been purchased under the VPP. It becomes very important, however, to follow Apple's guidance as to what version of VPP purchases should be chosen based on your use case. Also, you should be careful to not apply an app to a device if it has not been first put into the Supervise mode, as this will not allow you to reclaim the app code if you're relying on this method of app distribution.

While this is not necessarily pertinent for a security discussion, the online VPP portal from Apple provides an interface to download redemption codes for use with Apple Configurator, and it inquires internally how many of these have ever been applied to devices. The Apple Configurator interface helpfully provides feedback about how many have been redeemed per product and it provides a spreadsheet of codes as well. It may seem obvious, but do not use the same spreadsheet of codes with an MDM or other distribution methods.

# Mass restoring and naming of devices

From a branding or support standpoint, having the icons consistently arranged with a standard home screen background is desirable. Although MDMs are supposedly gaining this functionality, the original way to do these customizations, whether in the Prepare or Supervise modes, is to create a backup. (Backups made from a device in one mode cannot be restored to another with Apple Configurator.) This often requires manual interaction and if you have an MDM, it would make sense to allow it to perform any applicable configurations. It's very straightforward in the interface where you would initiate the creation of a backup when you are in either mode, and you can even access the stored backups.

Apple Configurator also protects the throughput of the USB bus by limiting concurrent operations to somewhere in the range of three at a time.

Note that the application is limited to 30 concurrent USB connections over a powered hub, which is obviously not the maximum for the protocol.

Also, keep in mind that except with very recent, specialized hardware, USB hubs can practically be considered addressless except for physical identification. The most reliable way to be confident that devices on a large hub are being named or otherwise prepared in a particular order is to attach each cable to the device in the sequence that you like.

Note that if you supervised a device and it is lost, stolen, or broken to the point that it cannot reconnect to Apple Configurator, you will lose any applicable app codes if you are using VPP. (Which is to say the original "redemption codes" version in comparison to the licenses model referred to in the VPP portal as "managed distribution", for use with MDM.) To reclaim the previously supervised device's name to keep your inventory neat, you can select it from the list in Apple Configurator and under the **Devices** menu, hold down the **Option** key. **Unsupervise** will change to **Remove** and you can prepare a new device to take that slot in the sequence. The same goes when a device is repaired and replaced with a device that has a different serial number, if you were not able to unsupervise the previous device before it left your possession.

# Backup concerns

When there is a supervision relationship between many of your devices and you realize that only small workgroups or sets of devices fit in the Apple Configurator usage model, backups become crucial, and alternatives to prevent over-reliance or an abundance of hacky workarounds become attractive. Taking backups as the first topic, Apple ships built-in backup software called Time Machine that can be used to protect the computer that runs Apple Configurator, but it is limited in its capabilities. You can either directly connect a hard drive (which can be encrypted), or send the backup over the local network to a machine running a compatible endpoint. It is not optimized for over-the-WAN offsite backup, among other shortcomings.

To separately understand the files in use, first we'll reprise our talk about sandboxing. In a rare reversal of the "do as I say, not as I do" maxim, Apple is following its own rules with Apple Configurator by using the container model for its data storage, which puts the files it operates with away from the view of the user. It is literally deep within a hidden folder. You can reach it by navigating to **Users** | CurrentUser (the current user's name) | **Library** | **Containers** | **com.apple.configurator** | **Data** | **Library**. Yes, the repetition is intentional.

Similar to Time Machine, Apple Configurator leverages links to refer to files outside of its sandbox for which it doesn't need write access. (Time Machine uses hard links to stub unchanged files from previous backups, which lets it present a complete set when you browse the most current folder structure in its storage destination.)

Another repeated pattern is the use of SQLite as the storage mechanism for the database of supervised devices and other inventory-related information. This is located in a subdirectory of the path listed earlier and you can go to it by navigating to **Application Support** | **com.apple.configurator** | **AppleConfigurator.storedata**. iOS software updates that are often full OS installations get cached within **Firmware** under **Caches** and apps imported into the program get stored in **Resources**, which you can reach by navigating to **Application Support** | **com.apple.configurator**.

# Configurator as chaperone

It is a common troubleshooting tip to turn up the verbosity of a process, look through the logs, and check any settings or configuration files. Mac folks have long gathered commands that enable hidden settings in preference files that are Apple-flavored XML files, just as we said were the case for configuration profiles. If you run `defaults write com.apple.configurator LogLevel ALL` (with the preference domain mapping to the path of `com.apple.configurator.plist` at **Preferences** by navigating to **Users** | `CurrentUser` (the current user's name)| **Library** | **Containers** | **com.apple.configurator** | **Data** | **Library**), you will cause informational text built into the debug output of the application to be written to logs. You can then sift through this information by viewing `system.log` in the Console application inside the **Utilities** folder in **Applications**, if you're running as an admin user on Mac. (Otherwise, you can tail the `system.log` file by navigating to **var** | **log** if you can elevate yourself to an admin user from a shell.)

Sometimes, old codenames for apps, devices, or features stick around in the inner workings of applications, and if you run defaults read on the preceding file (or open it in a binary `plist` compatible text editor such as Xcode), you'll notice the **ChaperoneCertificateIssuer** and **ChaperoneCertificateSerial** key/value pairs. Supervision may very well have used this Chaperone naming internally at Apple during development. Similarly, the name of the profile that Apple Configurator installs when supervising the device is referred to as **com.apple.configurator. chaperoneprofile**. The following screenshot shows the settings on a supervised device; this is an example of Apple Configurator's installed profile:

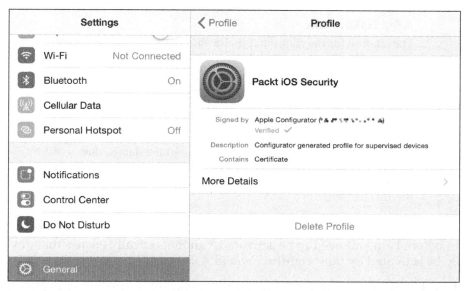

In **Settings** on a supervised device, this is an example of what Apple Configurator's installed profile looks like

In past versions of Apple Configurator, you would see that the console output also mentions the Boolean (true/false) value for the "chaperoned" property of a device that is being interacted with. This concept of a host having a responsibility relationship with the device helps further stress the importance of guarding the computer that is running Apple Configurator. If this machine is ever compromised, (or perhaps even worse, experiences data loss) you would be in quite a pickle indeed.

# Activation Lock and Find My iPhone

A boon for theft prevention (or a bust for the iOS device resale market), is the implementation of a new feature, as of iOS 7, by Apple called **Activation Lock**, which is an extension of iCloud's previous Find My iPhone feature. If you had an iCloud account configured with the setting on an iOS 7 device and it needed to be reactivated from scratch after a restore, the process would not have been able to proceed until that account's password was entered. This was felt to be a burden and a management headache for those who lent out devices regularly, but by some municipality's statistics, this alone reduced theft of iOS devices as they became practically useless.

**A few links to note**

The citation for the claim that thefts (and the iPhone resale market) are impacted by this feature can be found at http://arstechnica.com/apple/2014/06/ios-7-activation-lock-cutting-iphone-theft-damages-resale-market/.

Apple's **Check Activation Lock Status** page at https://www.icloud.com/activationlock/ for use before you buy or receive a phone.

Look at Apple's guidance on how to deal with a device that is still locked (http://support.apple.com/en-us/HT201441) or preparing your own device for sale (http://support.apple.com/en-us/HT201351).

Apple, as the central clearinghouse of devices that must come onto the network and check in before being allowed to be activated, can theoretically ensure that devices can only be activated by their rightful owners.

To address the problem of institutions that want control over whether customers can enable this feature and do not find it desirable when they'd like to reprovision the device to another user, two techniques exist. The first one is that an MDM can block Activation Lock until a bypass code can be generated for the device and sent to the service for a certain window of time after an enrollment that is akin to a full disk encryption key escrow, which provides a distinct, non-identifying "get out of jail free" card so that you can reactivate the device without the presence of the previous iCloud-identified user. You can find more details at http://support.apple.com/en-us/HT202804 in Apple's documentation about how they recommend folks mix tools such as an MDM or Apple Configurator into their support procedures around Activation Lock.

The reference implementation of MDM for Apple, the **Profile Manager** service in their OS X Server app, has specific documentation on the Activation Lock bypass code at

http://help.apple.com/profilemanager/mac/4.0/#/apd94BD5B2E-6448-450D-B76F-605AEEEEC9D7.

The other technique to deal with Activation Lock is that by default supervision does not allow this feature to be enabled in the first place. Are you getting the idea that Apple really wants you to supervise your devices? Only if you then use an MDM that enables the feature (via escrowing a bypass code or otherwise) can devices use the feature. Even if the end user enables Activation Lock on a supervised device, putting the device into *Recovery mode* will allow you to wipe (or prepare or refresh) it as you see fit. If you're given a device that was not supervised before Activation Lock was enabled, you will get an error message that says that it is "Unable to check iOS".

*Recovery mode* is a state where the device has booted to its firmware and has been told that it needs a fresh OS installation. It previously showed a Connect to iTunes message with a USB connector, but now it shows an arrow from a lightning connector to the new red iTunes icon (`http://support.apple.com/en-us/HT1212`). You can also use a utility like `RecBoot` or others if you often find yourself recovering a forgotten password, but be sure to carefully evaluate and inspect applications that purport to do cool things to iOS devices, as they are not officially sanctioned by Apple and may be from compromised sources (`http://jaxov.com/2010/05/recboot-iphone-recovery-mode/`). The following screenshot shows a prompt that displays the error encountered when you try to prepare a device with Activation Lock enabled:

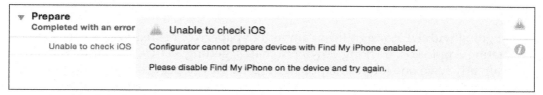

The error presented when you try to prepare a device with Activation Lock enabled

# Addressing the rough spots

For years, Apple said you could try a stick-and-carrot approach, using HR policy and enticements to stop end users from removing MDM or supervision profiles, with the ultimate caveat being that end users could always wipe the device. iOS 8 finally delivered a more comprehensive way to ensure that the devices are managed after being given to end users. Now, there is a restriction on access to the setting that erases all data and settings if the device is supervised, but only DEP, which we'll discuss later, truly keeps the device locked to your MDM. You can also restrict the removal of profiles by setting passwords as needed for removal in an ad hoc manner.

Between the small (intended) workgroup scale, inflexibility regarding interaction with things like backups, and the singular, fat client-based point of failure, many have hoped that there were other options. GroundControl is a new product that can provide some of the powerful features and functionality of Configurator without its limitations. (Disclaimer: one of our technical editors is the lead developer on this project.) This cloud-based solution aims to put tight control of the deployment process in the hands of the stakeholders. You can learn more about this at `https://www.groundctl.com`.

# DEP versus Apple Configurator

The **Device Enrollment Program (DEP)** is provided by Apple to alter the setup assistant so that devices can be unboxed by end users, but they are then forced to enroll into the MDM. DEP can also enable supervision without Apple Configurator. In fact, Apple recommends that you are not supposed to use devices that have DEP with Apple Configurator, at least while they are assigned to an MDM. Just as Activation Lock would cause trouble with Apple Configurator; DEP would like to kick in when the device is being activated, and this is not currently engineered into the product. Apple's documentation regarding the example use cases where DEP can be used with Apple Configurator is found at `http://support.apple.com/en-us/HT201092`.

To get going with DEP, a significant amount of paperwork is required such as associating Apple IDs, tracking down purchases, getting a D-U-N-S number if you don't already have one for your Apple Enterprise Developer account, and then connecting the DEP portal to your MDM. And even before all that, it may not be available in your country. The complete list of countries that have DEP can be found at `https://deploy.apple.com/qforms/open/register/country/aws`.

The actual moving parts for setting up DEP with your MDM are mostly concerned with what you want to see as part of the setup assistant. There is also the option to lock the MDM profile and enable supervision.

Keep in mind that things such as supervision and locking down devices shouldn't be a concern when you're only supporting a BYOD program. However, there are certainly many important considerations to keep in mind when you transition from previously deployed and supervised devices to DEP. Just like supervision, you must wipe the device so that it always points to your MDM during setup. This brings us to a bit of a show-stopper for many, and that is the fact that you are not supposed to restore the backup taken from the same device that is now being associated with DEP.

This makes it sound like there isn't a real migration path for pre-existing managed devices. We are not making this up. For more information, you can refer to `http://support.apple.com/en-us/HT202977`. You are even expected to MDM-wipe or Apple Configurator-unsupervise devices before they can be considered active within DEP. For moving data, the following choice quote is included under **Apple Configurator: Transitioning to Apple Deployment Programs**:

*When an iCloud backup is restored to the same device, all supervision and profiles come from the backup regardless of how it was configured in the Device Enrollment Program. For this reason, when restoring backups each user should transition to a new or different device to ensure Device Enrollment Program supervision and MDM enrollment are enforced.*

When we filed a radar (bug report) on this behavior, the response received "works as intended".

# Guided Access versus App Lock versus Single App Mode

The previous section on **Guided Access** in *Chapter 2, Introducing App Security*, introduced us to the concept of putting the device into a mode where very little can go wrong with it, but this also limits it to a single purpose — locking the device to run only one app. Note that this would only be applicable for supervised devices. Apple Configurator can be told which app to run and the device will bypass the home screen after the device is woken from sleep. The previous guidance applies for making sure that you can get access to the Apple Configurator station in case it needs maintenance, or to make sure that the network access is reliable if using Single App Mode with MDM. In addition, ensure that the power settings are applied, as end users would need to put the screen to sleep manually since they don't have access to settings.

As Single App Mode allows ad hoc, over-the-air application of the profile to make the device enter this locked-to-app mode, you can first allow end users to set a passcode on the device before the home screen becomes inaccessible. While this allows it to remain locked when unattended, make sure you consider apps that prompt for authentication and allow you to log out if sensitive data or systems are to be used.

# ActiveSync

You may get along very well without any of these tools that we've discussed so far. In addition, MDM is not particularly necessary if the ActiveSync protocol delivers the restrictions and security features that you need. The protocol was also adopted by paid versions of the Google Apps product and it is natively supported when you configure an Exchange e-mail account on iOS.

Many aspects of the server and Outlook Web Access interface work in exactly the same manner with iOS as they would with Blackberry, Symbian, Windows Mobile, Windows Phone, or an Android device. However, while the 14.0 version of the specification should be supported, the actual applicable settings have remained somewhat unchanged for years. Recently, Microsoft has been promoting various new products to manage mobile devices, which support the native management frameworks of each of the popular platforms.

As a refresher, management settings enforceable via the ActiveSync protocol are as follows:

- Wiping the device (if the device is lost or stolen)
- Enforcing a device passcode, with complexity, expiration, history, timeout before prompt, and failed attempt thresholds
- Allowing use of the camera (which was originally focused around courts or government-related buildings and contractors)
- Disabling sync while the device is roaming to help with data usage while you are outside normal cellular coverage

Further, via a configuration profile, you can limit how far in the past your mail is synced, along with other account-specific settings like certificates.

# Summary

Over the course of this chapter, we spent a lot of time investigating Apple Configurator. We discussed the Prepare mode, which can make lightweight, one-off changes as per your need. Supervision and user check out or assignment sets up long-term management "chaperone" relationships with iOS devices. We went over how Apple Configurator distributes the older version of VPP app codes and how it can lock the device into an app. As Activation Lock helped to make a device's theft become less effective, supervision also provided a safety net for institutions by allowing them to reclaim devices via the Recovery mode. We also reminded you that before evaluating an MDM, many restriction-related features are actually available to ActiveSync as an alternative.

For security professionals, it may seem like Apple is clueless about the needs of large enterprises, and Apple Configurator may not help with that impression. But by providing best practices we're left with the most supportable management, which works with the platform instead of against it. Apple has pushed the idea of "tier zero" or "the new IT" as a hands-off, infinitely scalable solution where IT lets end users perform maintenance tasks and it doesn't need to build walls between work and personal data in everyone's devices. We can do our best work when we are protecting devices by concentrating on how little of the device needs to be managed, even if they are owned by institutions. Even when it seems that the controls that are available aren't of industrial strength, practical concerns are going to trump a tightly locked-down experience. Apple, its customers, and its developers still need room to experiment and bring real innovation and productivity to mobile devices.

# 5
# Mobile Device Management

**Mobile Device Management (MDM)** refers to the technology that allows the centralized management of mobile devices, including those that run Apple's iOS. Centrally controlling iOS devices is an absolute requirement for many large organizations. Centralized management is also becoming a necessity in smaller environments. There are a lot of products that can be used to manage devices. These range from tools such as the inexpensive Profile Manager built into the Mac OS X `Server` application to third-party tools such as AirWatch, MaaS360 (by IBM), Mobile Iron JAMF's Casper Suite, and Bushel.

 In the interest of full disclosure, Bushel is being developed by one of the authors of this book. Bushel is represented here because of the depth of knowledge that the authors have of the product.

In this chapter, we will cover the following topics:

- Introducing MDM
- Using configurator versus mobile device management
- Profile Manager
- Introducing Bushel

These are meant to showcase the technology and are not an endorsement of any single solution. The reason that it's hard to endorse any single solution is that each has specific strengths and weaknesses, and each should be considered independently according to the environment.

# Introducing MDM

As mentioned, MDM is a technology that empowers you to centrally manage mobile devices. MDM's framework is developed by Apple and works using the **Apple Push Notification service** (**APNs**) to send messages from Apple. The notifications by the APNs do not actually contain commands or settings, but instead notify the device to look back at an MDM server, to pull commands that are waiting on the server.

MDM commands can wipe, lock, and perform other tasks on devices. MDM commands can also leverage profiles to configure settings on devices, similar to how we configured settings using **Apple Configurator** in this chapter. However, when configuring settings via an MDM solution, the profiles are installed over the air. This allows you to change settings daily or based on a device meeting a specific requirement. For example, with some third-party tools, you can wipe a device based on the geographic location of the device. MDM refers to the myriad of technologies that go into facilitating these transactions.

# Configurator versus MDM

In *Chapter 4, Organizational Controls*, we looked at managing devices locally using the Apple Configurator. The Apple Configurator works by installing profiles on devices using the USB connection from the computer to the devices. This works great in certain environments, such as when you just want to load settings onto a device prior to giving it out to a user. However, for a number of scenarios, you will want to update devices over the air. And, for a number of other scenarios, you need to use Apple Configurator or a combination of Apple Configurator and an MDM solution.

As mentioned, there are a number of tasks that cannot be managed using an MDM solution. These include the following:

- Restoring data to devices
- Setting the background image of devices
- Upgrading devices
- Enabling supervision, with the exception of Device Enrollment Program (DEP) devices (DEP allows Apple devices to be tied to an MDM solution)

Apple Configurator, on the other hand, can be used for all of the preceding points, as well as enrolling into an MDM solution. It can also be used to supervise devices without an MDM, the benefits of which we discussed in the previous chapter. This makes using Apple Configurator a viable use case for the tasks it can perform; it also helps to automate the setup of a lot of devices.

# The Profile Manager

There are a lot of providers with MDM solutions, such as Symantec, IBM, Sophos, JAMF Software, and others. We're going to use **Profile Manager** in this chapter, not because it's the best of them, but because it's an Apple product. The features of each MDM solution can be quickly and easily compared at http://www.enterpriseios. com/wiki/Comparison_MDM_Providers.

In this chapter, we will look at two solutions. The first is Apple's **Profile Manager**. This is a service included as part of the Server application, which runs on Mac OS X and is built by Apple. The Server app can be purchased from the Mac App Store for around 20 dollars (USD). However, the **Profile Manager** is not a complete solution for many; it lacks some scalability and ease of use that other vendors have built into their products. The second is a newcomer called Bushel. The **Profile Manager** requires an OS X Server, whereas Bushel is a SaaS solution.

# Preparing the Profile Manager Server

As mentioned, **Profile Manager** requires a Mac running OS X Server. In many cases, this server is a simple Mac mini server. Before we get started with installing the Server application and showing how to use **Profile Manager**, prepare the computer that will be used as the server.

 For testing, the server can be a virtual machine when running on Apple hardware.

Setting up the **Profile Manager** involves preparing the server by configuring a static IP address on the OS X Server. Once you have installed the Server app from the Mac App Store, configure a static IP address using the **Network System Preferences** pane. Once done, you will need to properly configure a hostname.

The hostname in this example will be `Yosemiteserver.krypted.com`. When initially set up, a self-signed certificate is installed. It's simple to generate a CSR and install a certificate from a **Certificate Authority (CA)**; however, doing so is beyond the scope of this example. Perform the following steps:

1. First, elevate your privileges by invoking `bash` with `sudo`:

   ```
   sudo bash
   ```

2. Next, configure the hostname using the `scutil` command:

   ```
   sudo scutil --set HostName Yosemiteserver.krypted.com
   ```

3. Then, configure the computer name using the `ComputerName` option with the `scutil` command:

   ```
   sudo scutil --set ComputerName Yosemiteserver
   ```

4. Finally, configure the local host name using the `LocalHostName` option with `scutil`:

   ```
   sudo scutil --set LocalHostName Yosemiteserver
   ```

> The preceding `ComputerName` and `LocalHostName` operations can be performed using the **Sharing System Preference** pane; however, we are doing it here since we are already in the command line and its one less screenshot to take up half a page.

Once the names are properly configured, check whether they function properly using the `changeip` command:

```
sudo changeip -checkhostname
```

The output of the `changeip` command should appear similar to the following example:

```
Primary address = 192.168.210.201
Current HostName = Yosemiteserver.krypted.com
DNS HostName = Yosemiteserver.krypted.com
The names match. There is nothing to change.
dirserv:success = "success"
```

If you're unsuccessful and don't see `success`, you may need to do some work to resolve the domain names:

1. When hosting your own DNS from within the **Server** app on the **Profile Manager** server, verify that the DNS server is set using the IP address used on the server.

2. When hosting a DNS on an Active Directory-based DNS server or other non-local DNS server, verify that you have properly working, forward and reverse records for the hostname and IP address combination in use on the OS X Server or the Active Directory integrated server.

3. From the **Server** app on the **Profile Manager** server or other Mac, click on the **Websites** service and then on the **ON** button (which would say **OFF** to start with). Don't configure anything else for the web server.

4. When the service starts, you will see the path to the default websites (`/Library/Server/Web/Data/Sites/Default`) and a **View Server Website link** will be displayed on the screen, as shown in the following figure:

The setup of the web service

Click on the **View Server Website** link at the bottom of the **Server** app. Then verify that the Welcome to OS X Server page loads. Doing so verifies that the web service (Apache) starts properly and is accessible.

# Preparing Profile Manager

Once you see the **Welcome to OS X Server** page, click on **Profile Manager** in the **Server** app sidebar. Then, click on the **Configure** button, shown in the following screenshot:

The **Profile Manager** Service

The **Configure Device Management** assistant appears. Click on the **Next** button.

Many environments will have an existing directory service that the **Profile Manager** server connects to. If you connect to Active Directory, then **Profile Manager** will require an **Open Directory** master or replica to be accessible. If there is none, then click on the **Create a New Open Directory** domain in the **Configure Network Users and Groups** screen (or go on to create the **Directory Administrator** account if prompted to do so instead). This directory service will be used for **Profile Manager**. If you have an existing directory service, then the existing service will be used for usernames and passwords and this one you just created will only be used for **Profile Manager**.

If you're creating an **Open Directory** domain, click on the **Next** button. Then, provide an administrative username and password for **Open Directory**. The default username is diradmin. Click on the **Next** button.

When prompted on the **Organization Information** screen, provide the name of your organization and an administrator's e-mail address (the e-mail address to put on certificates), as in the following screenshot, and then click on the **Next** button.

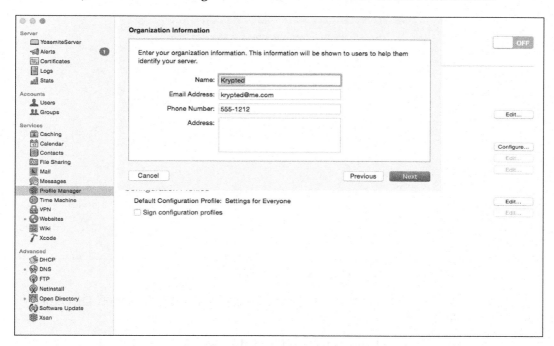

Providing an organization's information

The settings you used are then displayed on the **Confirm Settings** screen.

Click on the **Set Up** button. If prompted to do so, choose a certificate (the next screenshot) and then click on **Next**.

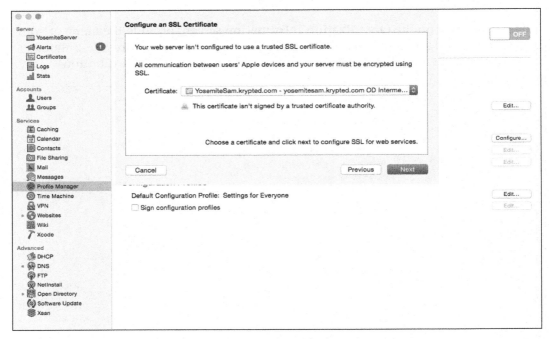

Configuring an SSL Certificate

For this example, we will use the self-signed certificate created by **Open Directory** and click on **Next**.

The APNs certificate establishes a trust relationship between Apple and your **Profile Manager** server so that push notifications can be sent to devices. You should use an institutional Apple ID for your organization (for example, apns@krypted.com) rather than a private one (for example, charlesedge@krypted.com). Once you have entered the credentials for a valid Apple ID, click on the **Next** button.

Provided the Apple ID authenticates and everything works as intended, click on the **Finish** button to complete and exit the configuration assistant. The **Configure** button should then be gone. Once back at the **Profile Manager** settings in **Server**, select **Sign Configuration Profiles**, displayed in the following screenshot:

Signing up your configuration profile

From the **Code Signing Certificate** sheet, choose the appropriate certificate, and click on the **OK** button:

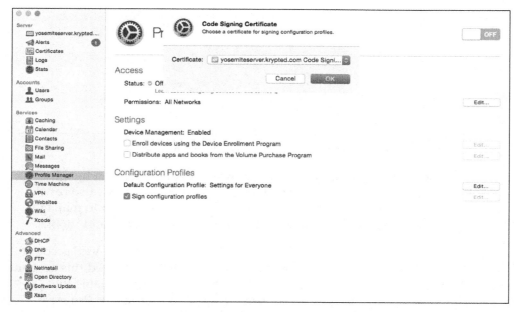

Choosing a code signing certificate

[ You can also import a certificate here if you have purchased a code-signing certificate. ]

# Completing Post Configuration tasks

Enable the **Include configuration for services** option to automatically build your configuration profile settings for services hosted on the server (Mail, Calendars, VPN, and so on). If you use the **Profile Manager** server for other services, leave this option enabled; otherwise, disable it as seen in the following screenshot.

Enabling configuration for services running on the server

Apple's **Volume Purchase Program** (**VPP**) allows you to buy apps on the Mac App Store or iOS App Store in bulk and distribute them to users. You can also revoke apps when employees leave your organization. VPP also allows you to manage iBooks as well. **Profile Manager** can help you distribute these apps and iBooks.

To enable the VPP features of **Profile Manager**, you will first need a VPP account, which can be obtained from deploy.apple.com. Once you have created this account, download your unique token file. Then, back in **Profile Manager**, enable the checkbox for **Distribute apps and books from the Volume Purchase Program**. Click on the **Choose** button and select the token file you downloaded earlier from Apple.

Once these apps are added, click on the **ON** slider (which would say **OFF** until clicked). Doing so starts the **Profile Manager** service. Once you see the URL to access your web interface, you can start managing devices using **Profile Manager**:

Accessing the **Profile Manager** service

Once the **Profile Manager** service is started, click on **Open Profile Manager** at the bottom of the **Profile Manager** settings screen. Authenticate yourself on the login page to manage your iOS and OS X devices.

# Using Profile Manager

Once you log in, there is a ton of options. You can configure policies for devices and placeholders and get lost pretty quickly. Hence, we're going to provide a primer on configuring profiles and managing devices. The easiest way to get started is to use the **Everyone** profile. This profile allows you to configure profiles for services running on the server to deploy settings to all users enrolled on the server.

The **Everyone** group has a **Restrictions** section, which allows administrators to restrict access to various **Profile Manager** options. These include restricting access to the **My Devices** portal (we'll cover using **My Devices** for enrollment later in this chapter), locking for devices (an option within **My Devices**), and the ability for users to wipe their own Apple device.

The DEP is a system that automatically configures Apple devices to join an MDM upon setup, which begins a process that users can complete. You can allow your users to automatically enroll via DEP here.

Activation Lock is a feature in iOS that restricts a device from being erased and reactivated without the Apple ID that was used to originally set up the Activation Lock features. This can be challenging if users do not actually own their devices. When running supervised devices, you can disable Activation Lock or generate a bypass code to unlock a device that has been locked through Activation Lock, as shown in the following screenshot:

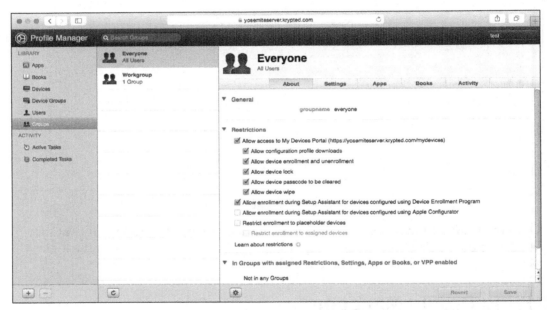

Logging in to **Profile Manager** for the first time

# Enrolling into Profile Manager

To manage a device, you must first enroll the device in **Profile Manager**. Enrollment is an opt-in procedure, unless the device is assigned to an MDM server via DEP. Use the URL of the server followed by My Devices to access the My Devices portal, which is how users can enroll their own devices into **Profile Manager**. This brings up a list of profiles that can be installed manually.

Enrolling devices in **Profile Manager**

Tap on the **Enroll** button to enroll a device. When prompted, tap on **Continue**:

Installing profiles

You will receive an error if you are installing a certificate that hasn't yet been trusted by a third-party **Certificate Authority (CA)**. As can be seen in the following screenshot, click on the **Install** button:

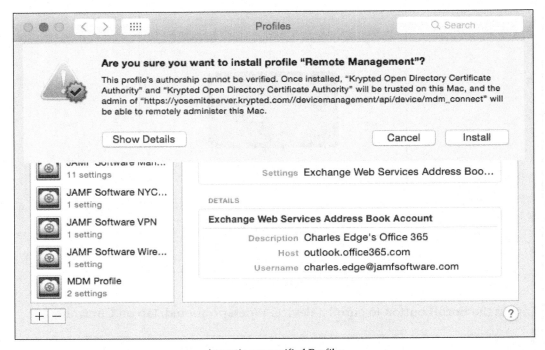

Accepting unverified Profiles

Once you're enrolled, click on **Profile** in the **Profiles** section of the **Settings** app to see what settings are deployed and optionally unenroll devices. Users can wipe or lock their own devices from the **My Devices** portal or administrators can manage devices from the administrative portal.

# Device management

As mentioned, you can then manage iOS devices from **Profile Manager**. The first task we'll cover here is enforcing a passcode policy for a group of devices. To do so, click on **Device Groups** in **Profile Manager** and select a group of devices.

A critical aspect of any management solution is to see the inventory information. The information shown includes certificates installed by the MDM solution, UDID, Last Checkin Time, Wi-Fi MAC, Ethernet MAC addresses, Device Model, and whether the personal hotspot is enabled. You can also see the apps that the MDM solution has installed and the restrictions that have been enforced by the MDM solution.

# Passcode policies

Real-time management of devices is done using the **Devices** screen. Here, we can access machine-specific information and settings using the Settings (cog) button, as well as wipe and lock devices. Try to always use groups to deploy policies, as we do here. From **Device Groups**, select your group and then click on the **Settings** tab. Click on the **Edit** button shown in the next screenshot:

Device Groups

Since we're configuring a passcode policy, click on **Passcode.** The items in the left column are known as payloads. Click on **Configure to setup the passcode payload**. Check the box and enable **Allow simple value**, as shown in the following screenshot. Then, set the **Minimum passcode length** option to a number. We really like using four characters. Then, click on the **OK** button to save your changes.

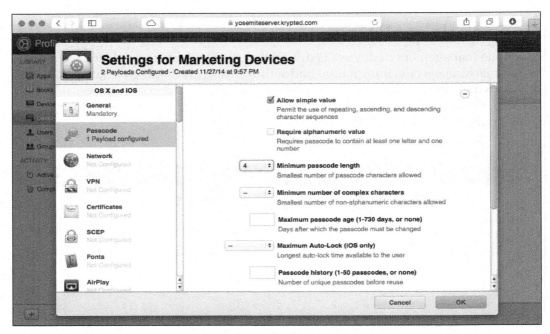

Configuring passcode requirements

Okay! That didn't save your changes to the profile, only to that payload within the profile. Click on the **Save** button on the **Save Changes?** screen to finish the process. You'll know everything worked when the device prompts you for a new passcode if one is already configured.

Wiping a device is another common administrative task. Make sure you're using a device where you don't mind losing *everything* before you follow along with this example. To wipe a device, select the device from **Profile Manager** and then click on the Settings (cog) button, as you did earlier. This time, click on **Wipe**:

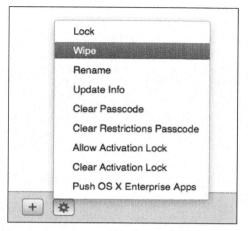

Wiping a device

When the **Wipe** screen comes up, click on **Wipe**. Because this is destructive to data on the device, you'll be prompted to click on **Wipe** a second time. If you look at your device, note that it should instantly go black, and then, reboot the device.

 If the device is DEP-enabled, it will automatically begin the enrollment process again once it joins a Wi-Fi network for the first time.

# Introducing Bushel

In the interest of full disclosure, one of the authors of this book works at JAMF Software, the company that makes **Bushel**. It is a very simple, easy-to-use MDM that allows us to showcase, using a third-party solution, to make changes on devices using the fewest number of screenshots so we can fit them into this book.

# Setup

You can set up a Bushel account from `signup.bushel.com`. When prompted for your company name, provide it a subdomain name as well, as shown in the following screenshot:

Configuring your organization in Bushel

When the form is filled out, click on **Next**.

On the initial screen, provide your name, e-mail address, and a password, as shown in the next screenshot. The administrative username for the account will then be this e-mail address. Click on the **Create Account** button:

Configuring your Bushel account settings

You will receive an e-mail from Bushel. Click on the **Activate** button in the e-mail. Click on **Get Started** and then provide the mail settings for your domain or click on the **Skip** button to provide the APNs certificate so that you can enroll iOS devices into your Bushel account, as shown below in the following screenshot:

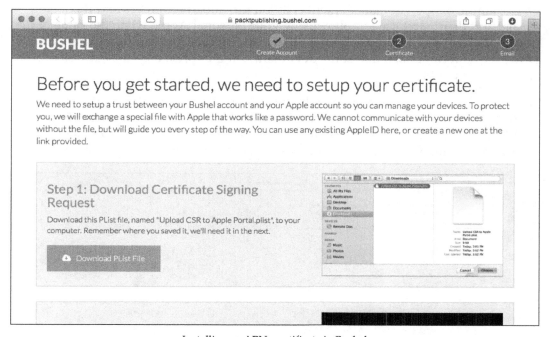

Installing an APNs certificate in Bushel

# The enrollment process

The enrollment process is similar to **Profile Manager** and other third-party MDM tools. Log into your Bushel account, click on **Enrollment**, and when prompted to **Enroll This Device**, click on the **Enroll** button. When prompted **Who will this device belong to?** enter the username (that is the user's name in front of their e-mail address, most likely, or the username for your e-mail system).

Provide the e-mail address as well, and then click on **Enroll This Device**. To enroll the device, use the default settings at each screen. You can also save the mobileconfig file downloaded (if using a Mac) and e-mail or text it to allow a user to enroll without visiting a website. You will need to leave the username field blank if you're distributing a profile to multiple people.

# Restrictions

Apple built a feature called **open in management** in iOS. This feature protects company data in mail accounts, apps, and even Safari links distributed by an MDM.

One example of open in management is if you download **Numbers** and **Box** using Bushel and then purchase Dropbox using your personal Apple ID on the same device, you can then open a document that came in through Numbers using Box. However, you can't open that same document using Dropbox, because it was not supplied via the MDM service.

Bushel enables open in management by default on all accounts. The button says **Protect corporate data on iOS devices**. To verify that open in management is enabled, click on the **Setup** tab. Then, click on **Security** in the sidebar and look for **Protect corporate data on iOS devices**, as seen in the following screenshot:

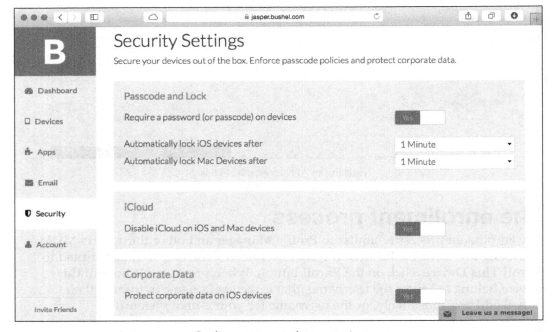

Configure corporate data protection

Make sure you are using VPP to deploy your apps and verify that the iOS device is using the mail account deployed via your MDM, rather than a manually configured account. To check the mail account, open **Settings**, tap on **Mail**, and verify that the settings found there cannot be changed. We will cover the **Volume Purchasing Program** in the next section.

# Volume Purchasing Program and MDM

**VPP** is a service provided by Apple that allows organizations to purchase apps in volume. Apps purchased in VPP and deployed through an MDM solution can also containerize data to only exchange data with apps deployed by that MDM solution. To deploy an app, simply click on **Apps** in the sidebar. If you have a .vpptoken file (a file you get from the Apple VPP portal), then you will see the apps purchased using the Apple VPP portal in your Library, as shown here:

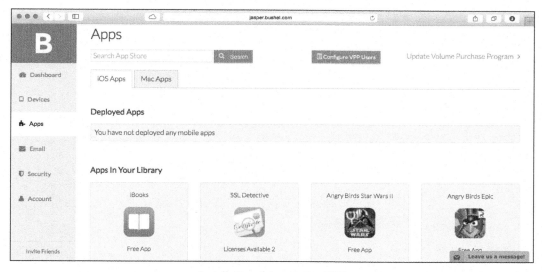

Installation of Apps using VPP

Click on an app and then click on the **Install** button to deploy the app to all devices enrolled in your Bushel account. Then try to copy data out of that app into the one manually installed from the App Store. Provided the copy fails, you have successfully built a walled garden for your app-based data.

# Summary

We did a lot in this chapter, which is great. In *Chapter 1, iOS Security Overview*, we looked at configuring passcodes, and in *Chapter 2, Introducing App Security*, we looked at app data. Here, we managed both with very basic policies, deployed by inexpensive and easy-to-use MDMs. You can get a lot of complicated functionalities with your MDM, if you choose. You can also do much more with the tools we provided in this chapter, so we hope you will explore everything these tools (and the other third-party MDM suites) have to offer.

In the next chapter, we'll conclude the book by turning our attention to the insides of the device, diving into debugging tools so you can dive even deeper into the abyss, that is, reverse engineering how these things work.

# 6
# Debugging and Conclusion

Every environment is different. Understanding the internal workings of an iOS device enables you to isolate items that you might consider to be a security threat for your particular environment that we haven't identified in this book. In addition, learning more about these devices is just plain cool! In this chapter, we're going to look at debugging and forensic data collection. These both showcase what kind of data can be pulled off from devices and teaches you more about the devices that you're securing.

As we've showcased throughout this book, Apple does a good job of protecting sensitive data on devices. In addition, application vendors have a lot of tools to keep your data secure as well. However, computers being what they are, some data can be obtained from them. In this chapter, we're going to cover the following topics:

- Xcode
- Diving deeper into `libimobiledevice`
- App communications such as identifying devices and network communications
- Apple IDs and Apps

We'll be going through the common tools for debugging iOS, reverse engineer to see how things run under the hood, and leverage that data for various use cases. This process starts with the tool that Apple provides for writing apps and this is called **Xcode**.

# Xcode

Xcode is written and distributed for OS X by Apple. Xcode is used to write apps for both OS X and iOS and it can be used to write scripts in various languages. Xcode also comes with a suite of tools that can be used to debug the apps that you're writing. These tools can also be used to view logs and watch what happens on devices when you're using them.

Xcode is available on the Mac App Store at https://itunes.apple.com/us/app/ xcode/id497799835?mt=12, as you can see in the following screenshot:

Install Xcode from the Mac App Store

In order to install Xcode from the Mac App Store, perform the following steps:

1. Click on **Install** and wait for the installation to complete to get Xcode installed on your computer.

2. Once installed, open **Xcode** from the **/Applications** directory.

3. Choose **Devices** from the **Window** menu to see a list of devices that the computer can connect to.

4. Plug in the device.

5. Click on your device to see basic information about the device and then click on the **View Device Logs** button to view the device logs, as shown in the following screenshot.

The Xcode **DEVICES** screen

> Note that at the bottom left of the **Device Information** pane is a Show/Hide button. Clicking on this displays the console of the connected device in real time.

6. The logs are then displayed. When they are reviewed, these logs provide a wealth of information about devices, as you can see in the next screenshot.

7. Right-click on a log and you can delete it from the device within Xcode. When you unplug the device, the log window closes.

 Note that you can also obtain Xcode from the Developer portal of Apple if you would rather not use the Mac App Store to do so.

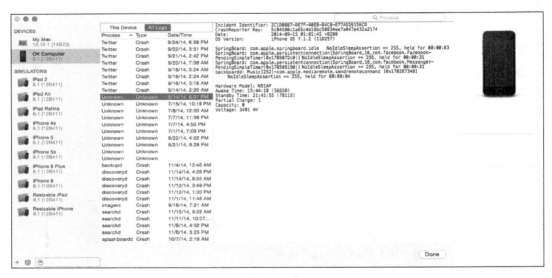

iOS Device Logs

Many of the same logs can be viewed from different Apple devices by opening the **Settings** app from the home screen, tap on **Privacy**, tapping on **Diagnostics & Usage**, and then tap on **Diagnostics & Usage Data**. From here, you can tap on entries to see the same debugging information that is available in Xcode, as shown in the following screenshot:

Diagnostics and usage data

# Dive deeper with libimobiledevice

Xcode and other tools can be used to view logs on iOS devices. Another tool that is used to debug devices is called libimobiledevice. This is an open source project that is meant to help security researchers, developers, and administrators track the goings-on of iOS devices. The libimobiledevice library is available at http://www.libimobiledevice.org

# Installing libimobiledevice using Homebrew

I usually install libimobiledevice using Homebrew, as there are a few dependencies that can be a little annoying to install otherwise.

To install Homebrew if you haven't already done so, perform the following steps:

1.  Elevate your privileges by running sudo and invoking a bash shell:

    ```
    sudo bash
    ```

2.  Run the following command:

    ```
    ruby -e "$(curl -fsSL https://raw.githubusercontent.com/Homebrew/
    install/master/install)"
    ```

3.  Once the command is executed, follow the prompts to complete the installation. Once Homebrew is installed, run the following brew command to download the required components and then libimobiledevice:

    ```
    brew install -v --fresh automake autoconf libtool wget
    libimobiledevice
    ```

4.  Then, run ideviceinstaller:

    ```
    brew install -v --HEAD --fresh --build-from-source
    ideviceinstaller
    ```

# Using idevicesyslog and idevicepair

Once these pair of tools are installed, you can plug in a paired device, unlock it, and use the following command to view the logs on the screen:

```
Idevicesyslog
```

This is akin to running a tail against the device. Again, the device must be paired. You can use the command line (for example, if you're running this on Linux) to view the logs, but if you're not paired, you'll need to use idevicepair to pair your device, followed by the pair verb (which is very different from the pear verb):

```
idevicepair pair
```

You can also unpair a device using the unpair command:

```
idevicepair unpair
```

When pairing and unpairing, you should see the appropriate entries in /var/db/lockdown.

# Using idevicedate and ideviceinstaller

The next option is `date` (very useful when scripting unit tests using this suite). To obtain this, use the `idevicedate` command; you do not need any operators or verbs:

```
idevicedate
```

Next, let's check the apps installed on a device. We can do this with the ideviceinstaller command (that is also part of the `ilibmobiledevice` suite of tools). Here, we'll use the `-l` option to just list what's installed:

```
/usr/local/bin/ideviceinstaller -l
```

The output would show the app along with the version of the app currently installed on the device:

```
com.apple.Pages - Pages 1716
```

To uninstall one of the listed apps, use the `--uninstall` option:

```
ideviceinstaller --uninstall com.protogeo.Moves
```

You can also install apps, provided you've cached the IPA file (for example, via iTunes):

```
ideviceinstaller --install /Users/charlesedge/Music/iTunes/iTunes\ Media/
Mobile\ Applications/Box\ 3.3.0.ipa
```

 Note that the preceding folder may change based on the operating system on which your library began with.

The preceding command returns the following output:

```
Copying '/Users/charlesedge/Music/iTunes/iTunes Media/Mobile
Applications/Box 3.3.0.ipa' to device... DONE.
Installing 'net.box.BoxNet'
Install - CreatingStagingDirectory (5%)
Install - ExtractingPackage (15%)
Install - InspectingPackage (20%)
Install - TakingInstallLock (20%)
Install - PreflightingApplication (30%)
Install - VerifyingApplication (40%)
Install - CreatingContainer (50%)
Install - InstallingApplication (60%)
Install - PostflightingApplication (70%)
Install - SandboxingApplication (80%)
Install - GeneratingApplicationMap (90%)
Install - Complete
```

When it is run against a device, the app can then open other apps, provided the user the Apple ID owns the app.

A provisioning profile is a profile that is used to install apps. These apps are usually located on a mail server that supports the ipa MIME type and the profile defines the location to obtain the app. This forms the basis of the Wirelurker attack, where attackers replace an app by spoofing the domain of the app. There's also a command for ideviceprovision that can be used to view installed provisioning profiles when they are run with the list verb:

```
/usr/local/bin/ideviceprovision list
```

As mentioned earlier, the ideviceprovision command can also install a provisioning profile; therefore it can actually make the device install an app. This is done using the ideviceprovision command followed by the install verb and the name (and path if the .mobileprovision file isn't in the working directory from where you're running the command) of the file that is being installed:

```
/usr/local/bin/ideviceprovision install angrybirds.mobileprovision
```

You can also remove the path of the working directory by feeding in the UUID of the provisioning profile that is obtained by using the list verb and replacing MYUUID from the following code block:

```
/usr/local/bin/ideviceprovision remove MYUUID
```

You can also put a device in recovery mode so that it would need to be plugged into a computer that is running iTunes and get a new ipsw file installed, which is as simple as feeding the UDID into ideviceenterrecovery:

```
/usr/local/bin/ideviceenterrecovery
af36e5d7065d4ad666bf047b6e4de26dd144578c
```

This brings up an interesting question. How would you get the UDID? You can use ideviceinfo to get this:

```
ideviceinfo
```

The preceding ideviceinfo output shows more information about a device than what I knew you could actually get previously. You can use grep for UniqueDeviceID as follows:

```
ideviceinfo | grep UniqueDeviceID | awk '{ print $2}'
```

This would just return the UDID. Since this is blank when no device is connected to the system, you can run a loop that waits for a few seconds when the UDID is empty and then uses that UDID as a $1 in some scripts. Of course, it's much easier to use a command that was built for this, which is called idevice_id:

```
idevice_id -l
```

Next, you can use `idevicediagnostics` to obtain some information about the current state of the device:

```
idevicediagnostics diagnostics All -u
af36e5d7065d4ad666bf047b6e4de26dd1445789
```

The `idevicediagnostics` command has an XML output with information about the device, such as how much battery life is still there. You can also query the `ioreg` file of the device, which shows what's plugged into the device:

```
idevicediagnostics ioreg IODeviceTree -u
af36e5d7065d4ad666bf047b6e4de26dd1445789
```

The `idevicediagnostics` command can also do some basic tasks (where each task is sent as a verb without the required UDID) such as restart, sleep, and shutdown:

```
idevicediagnostics restart
```

The crash reports on a device (which include reports of uninstalled apps that forensically provide a glimpse into what apps were removed from a device and when they were removed) can be extracted from a paired device as well, using `idevicecrashreport`:

```
idevicecrashreport -e /test
```

 The preceding directory must exist prior to executing the command and the current user must have permission to write.

You can then view the logs or `grep` through them for specific pieces of information:

```
cat /Test/Baseband/log-bb-2014-08-06-stats.plist
```

The last command that we're going to cover in this section is `idevicebackup2`, which is used to back up devices. Here, we're going to feed the UDID to it. I'm lazily using the `idevice_id` command from earlier, in back ticks, to grab the UDID and back it up in that `/test` directory when the device is unlocked.

```
idevicebackup2 -u `idevice_id -l` backup /test
```

Here, we've backed up whatever device is plugged into the `/test` directory. The subsequent backups will be incremental.

As you can see, there are a number of tasks that can be performed on a device when the device has been paired to a computer. This further emphasizes the fact that you should never pair your device to an untrusted computer.

You can also use the information obtained from these commands to troubleshoot and research a wide variety of things with regards to devices based on iOS. Having a backup, crash reports, and real-time logs, and making changes such as installing apps on devices allows you to do regression testing, vulnerability research, and a lot more in general that you wouldn't be able to do otherwise.

# App communications

Up until now, this chapter focused on viewing data on devices, obtaining logs, and making changes to devices themselves. Since listening to network traffic is the basis of most of the reconnaissance that is done on devices, we'll look at how to obtain more information about devices that are based on what goes over the network medium. This is done by first identifying the iOS devices on a network and then listening to raw network traffic using common tools such as Wireshark.

## Identifying devices

For starters, you can identify all iOS devices easily as they listen on port 62078, which is a unique port. To verify that an iOS device is occupying an IP on a network, scan the IP address for that port. For example, here we use the built-in port scanner in OS X to scan an IP address on the network with an iPhone:

```
/System/Library/CoreServices/Applications/Network\ Utility.app/Contents/
Resources/stroke 192.168.0.12 62078 62078
```

## Listening to network communications

OS X has a command called `rvictl` that can be used to proxy network communications from iOS devices through a computer over what's known as a **Remote Virtual Interface (RVI)**. To set up an RVI, you'll need the UDID of a device and the device will need to be plugged into a Mac and have the device paired to the Mac. This may seem like a lot, but if you've followed what we have been doing until now, this should be pretty simple.

To set up an RVI, we'll perform the following steps:

1.  First, we'll pair a device using the following command:

    ```
    idevicepair pair
    ```

2.  Then, we'll tap on **Trust** on the device itself. Then, we'll grab that UDID with `idevice_id`:

    ```
    idevice_id -l
    ```

3. Next, we'll set up an RVI with `rvictl` and the `-s` option (here I'm just going to grab the UDID since I only have one device plugged into my computer):

```
rvictl -s `idevice_id -l`
```

4. Then, we can list the connections using `rvictl` with the `-l` option:

```
rvictl -l
```

5. Next, we'll run a `tcpdump` command using this newly constructed `rvi0`:

```
tcpdump -n -i rvi0
```

6. Next, we'll get a lot of logs. Let's fire up the Nike `FuelBand` app and refresh our status. While watching the resultant traffic, we'll see a line like this:

```
22:42:29.485691 IP 192.168.0.12.57850 > 54.241.32.20.443: Flags
[S], seq 3936380112, win 65535, options [mss 1460,nop,wscale
5,nop,nop,TS val 706439445 ecr 0,sackOK,eol], length 0
```

There's an IP in this line—`54.241.32.20`. We can look this up and we'll be able to see that the servers are sitting on Amazon Web Services, and on verifying it, we come to know that it's Nike. By watching the traffic with `tcpdump`, we can obtain GET, POST, and other information that is sent and received. Using Wireshark, we can get even more detailed data.

Overall, this book is meant to focus on the iOS side of information security and not on debugging and refining the approach to using `tcpdump`/`wireshark`. The `rvictl` tool is a great tool in the iOS development cycle and for security researchers who are looking into the number of the apps on iOS devices that exchange data.

> While I've found that `rvictl` is able to show me pretty much anything I need access to, if you find any issues with it, go to `https://github.com/libimobiledevice/usbmuxd`. This is an open source project that is being developed more aggressively and can be used to do similar tasks.

# Apple IDs and Apps

One item that is not often covered when considering iOS security is the Apple ID that is used to manage a device. The Apple ID can potentially be used to wipe a device (for example, via the **Find My iPhone** app), restore a device's backup, or even view the purchased media (songs, movies, iBooks, and apps) that may not be available on a device.

When you uninstall an app, the app is still in your purchase history. As you can see in the following screenshot, you can get a fair amount of information about what someone uses a device for:

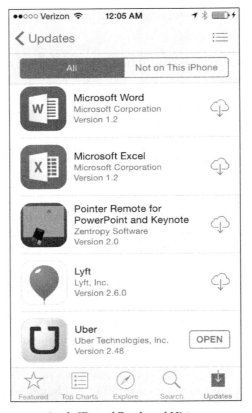

Apple IDs and Purchased History

The only way to prevent someone from looking at such information is to secure the Apple ID. Use strong passwords for these and change them from time to time. When an employee leaves an organization, you might also be able to reset their password using an e-mail address if the Apple ID uses a corporate e-mail address.

# Forensics

So far, we've discussed looking at data on devices. When you use a device, unless you made a forensic image of the device prior to using it, you are tainting evidence. This is not a book on forensics, but we can let you know about some tools that will allow you to acquire a forensically sound image of a device without much fanfare.

 Many of these tools are only available to law enforcement professionals. Apple has recently gone to great lengths to make their devices "leak" less data, even to law enforcement. Since iOS 7, it's been practically impossible to brute force passcodes and after Apple fixed the bootroom exploits of iPhone 4/iPad 2, it's no longer possible to obtain an image of the device's flash storage for offline analysis.

The following links are available to help you properly acquire evidence from iOS devices and computers that access iOS devices:

- iOS Forensic Toolkit: `http://www.elcomsoft.com/eift.html`
- Mobilyze: `https://www.blackbagtech.com/mobilyze.html`
- Access Data Forensic Toolkit: `http://www.elcomsoft.com/ios-forensic-toolkit.html`
- Lantern: `http://katanaforensics.com/forensics/lantern-v2-0/`
- Blacklight: `https://www.blackbagtech.com/forensics/blacklight/blacklight.html`
- iPhone Backup Analyzer: `http://ipbackupanalyzer.com/`
- Oxygen: `http://www.oxygen-forensic.com/en/`
- Forensic Hardware: `http://www.cellebrite.com/`
- iXAM: `http://www.ixam-forensics.com/devices.asp/`
- SecureView: `http://mobileforensics.susteen.com/`

 Many of these tools can also brute force passwords that are used on devices. However, this might be a lengthy process.

A basic tool that doesn't require to be purchased through law enforcement but can interact directly with a device is iExplorer from Macroplant. This tool does not expose items that are in secure enclaves on the device, but it allows you to have a lot more access than what you would otherwise have. iExplorer allows you to view Contacts, Messages, Notes, Safari's history, backups, and some app data. As you can see in the following screenshot, once it is installed, you can view Safari's browsing history:

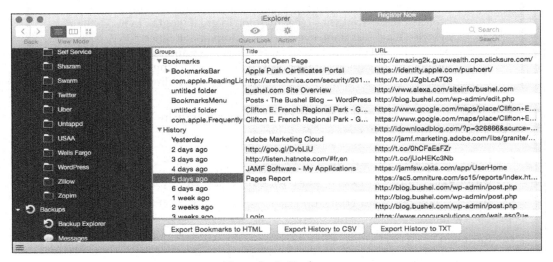

Macroplant's iExplorer

As you can see in the following screenshot, you can also view books and other forms of media in the folders in which these items are stored on the device. A user can access these folders without jailbreaking a device.

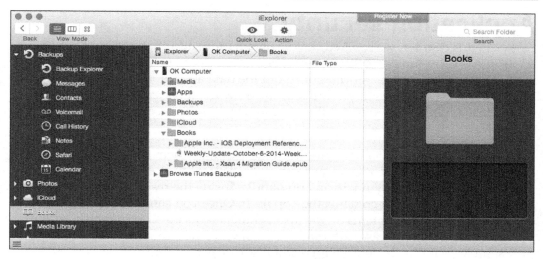

Viewing iBooks Data

To go further into a device and view preferences, operating system files, and so on, you will need to jailbreak it and use a tool such as iFunBox or iFile via Cydia, which is an app store for jail-broken devices. iFunBox is a Mac/Windows tool for examining the device's filesystem and iFile is an app that you can install on jail-broken devices. Since iOS7, you'll need to install a hacked **Apple File Conduit (AFC2)** from Cydia on a jail-broken device to access anything outside the normal sandboxed AFC areas of the device. (See `https://cydia.saurik.com/info/com.saurik.afc2d/` for more information on this.)

 For more information on jailbreaking devices, search for the term `Jailbreak` and also provide the model of device you have on Google. A lot of sites on jailbreaking come and go, so we're not going to include a link here, but it's worth checking out how people go about such things and the limitations on devices once they're jail-broken.

# Application security

Earlier in this chapter, we covered how to obtain more information about how applications communicate with servers. Here, we're going to take a brief look at how you can obtain more information about the data and/or binaries within an app. In apps, these are usually compiled, so you will not typically see raw source code. Most application vendors will not provide you with access to their source code either.

IPA files are zipped application bundles. You can unzip them before attempting to disassemble the binary. To do so, you can right-click on an IPA file and open it with **Archive Utility** to quickly unzip an app bundle. Inside the resulting folder, you'll see a `Payload` folder that contains the app itself. Once you can see the app, you can view the package contents on the app bundle and locate the binary file within. Unfortunately, in many cases although you can view the strings, attempting to disassemble an iOS app binary with a tool like Hopper can be fruitless because apps from the App Store are usually encrypted.

Ad hoc and enterprise distribution apps can be examined with these tools; however, many enterprise app developers use obfuscation techniques or wrappers to reduce the usefulness of disassembly on their production binaries.

In summary, these disassembly techniques probably aren't useful to the reader in any meaningful way. Unless you are an experienced developer with some assembly language knowledge, disassembly of even a simple unencrypted binary of any sort isn't likely to help you learn anything.

# Viewing an App

There are a number of tools that can help you to obtain more information about an app. You can use a command line to view the contents of a file, and when it is compiled, there's still a fair amount of information that can be derived from an iOS application file (an IPA file). To do this, simply use the `cat` command for a file from your app library:

```
Cat /Users/charlesedge/Music/iTunes/iTunes\ Media/Mobile\ Applications/
Amex\ 4.6.0.ipa
```

You can also view data in the file without all the special characters using the strings command:

```
Strings /Users/charlesedge/Music/iTunes/iTunes\ Media/Mobile\
Applications/Amex\ 4.6.0.ipa
```

There are also disassemblers that have different levels of luck in obtaining information about a file. For example, Hopper Disassembler that can be purchased from the Mac App Store at `https://itunes.apple.com/us/app/hopper-disassembler/id422856039?mt=12`. The following screenshot shows the Hopper Disassembler:

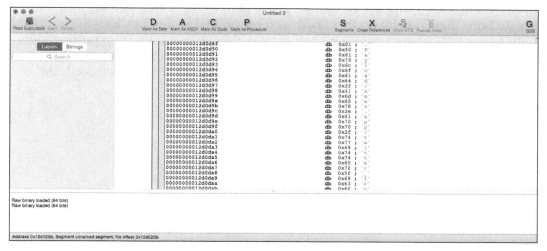

Hopper Disassembler

There's also a tool called **Clutch**, which is available on GitHub at `https://github.com/KJCracks/Clutch`. Clutch must be run from a jail-broken device, so it requires a somewhat thought-out method to decompile code; however, it is able to obtain more data than any other tool that we've seen.

There are many books that are available online that can help you to understand native programming languages if you aren't already aware of them.

# Summary

There are a number of places where we stopped ourselves from writing more in this chapter. This chapter does not provide in-depth information about packet capturing, forensic acquisition, application development, or iOS systems internals. Instead, similar to the rest of the book, we are pointing you towards the necessary content to do more if you choose.

The authors of this book are strong proponents of the hacker mentality. There really isn't more security information about devices that are available without jailbreaking devices or accessing Apple's Developer portal at `http://developer.apple.com`. We do hope that you will do them both at some point. We don't believe that you can fully secure a jail broken device, so you should, therefore, refrain from putting them into production. However, we also believe in learning as much as we can, which means eventually jailbreaking a device and seeing what really makes those little Speak-and-Spell apps tick.

# Index

## Thank you for buying
# Learning iOS Security

## About Packt Publishing

Packt, pronounced 'packed', published its first book, *Mastering phpMyAdmin for Effective MySQL Management*, in April 2004, and subsequently continued to specialize in publishing highly focused books on specific technologies and solutions.

Our books and publications share the experiences of your fellow IT professionals in adapting and customizing today's systems, applications, and frameworks. Our solution-based books give you the knowledge and power to customize the software and technologies you're using to get the job done. Packt books are more specific and less general than the IT books you have seen in the past. Our unique business model allows us to bring you more focused information, giving you more of what you need to know, and less of what you don't.

Packt is a modern yet unique publishing company that focuses on producing quality, cutting-edge books for communities of developers, administrators, and newbies alike. For more information, please visit our website at www.packtpub.com.

## About Packt Open Source

In 2010, Packt launched two new brands, Packt Open Source and Packt Enterprise, in order to continue its focus on specialization. This book is part of the Packt Open Source brand, home to books published on software built around open source licenses, and offering information to anybody from advanced developers to budding web designers. The Open Source brand also runs Packt's Open Source Royalty Scheme, by which Packt gives a royalty to each open source project about whose software a book is sold.

## Writing for Packt

We welcome all inquiries from people who are interested in authoring. Book proposals should be sent to author@packtpub.com. If your book idea is still at an early stage and you would like to discuss it first before writing a formal book proposal, then please contact us; one of our commissioning editors will get in touch with you.

We're not just looking for published authors; if you have strong technical skills but no writing experience, our experienced editors can help you develop a writing career, or simply get some additional reward for your expertise.

## Mobile Security: How to Secure, Privatize, and Recover Your Devices

ISBN: 978-1-84969-360-8          Paperback: 242 pages

Keep your data secure on the go

1. Learn how mobile devices are monitored and the impact of cloud computing.

2. Understand the attacks hackers use and how to prevent them.

3. Keep yourself and your loved ones safe online.

## Core Data iOS Essentials

ISBN: 978-1-84969-094-2          Paperback: 340 pages

A fast-paced, example-driven guide to data-driven iPhone, iPad, and iPod Touch applications

1. Covers the essential skills you need for working with Core Data in your applications.

2. Particularly focused on developing fast, lightweight, data-driven iOS applications.

3. Builds a complete example application. Every technique is shown in context.

4. Completely practical with clear, step-by-step instructions.

Please check **www.PacktPub.com** for information on our titles

## iPhone User Interface Cookbook

ISBN: 978-1-84969-114-7      Paperback: 262 pages

A concise dissection of Apple's iOS user interface design principles

1. Learn how to build an intuitive interface for your future iOS application.

2. Avoid app rejection with detailed insight into how to best abide by Apple's interface guidelines.

3. Written for designers new to iOS, who may be unfamiliar with Objective-C or coding an interface.

## iOS 5 Essentials

ISBN: 978-1-84969-226-7      Paperback: 252 pages

Harness iOS 5's new powerful features to create stunning applications

1. Integrate iCloud, Twitter, and AirPlay into your applications.

2. Lots of step-by-step examples, images and diagrams to get you up to speed in no time with helpful hints along the way.

3. Each chapter explains iOS 5's new features in-depth, whilst providing you with enough practical examples to help incorporate these features in your apps.

Please check **www.PacktPub.com** for information on our titles

CPSIA information can be obtained
at www.ICGtesting.com
Printed in the USA
LVOW03s0008140516
488228LV00008B/248/P